MW01097293

THE TSAR'S TREASURE

The Tsar's Treasure

The Sunken White Star Liner
With a
Billion Dollar Secret

Captain Martin Bayerle
&
G.S. Payne

First Edition
First Printing

LIBRARY OF CONGRESS PCN: 9780988876002

Printed in the United States of America on acid-free paper

Published by Barnburner Books, LLC
www.barnburnerbooks.com

Book Design & Formatting by Grant Edward

For Great-Uncle Will,
who taught me that an opposing wind
is essential for a kite to fly.
The stronger the wind,
the higher the flight.

TABLE OF CONTENTS

"[The] truth is incontrovertible. Panic may resent it, ignorance may deride it, malice may distort it, but there it is."

— Sir Winston Churchill

INTRODUCTION

This is the true story of a luxury ocean liner, deemed practically unsinkable, that now lies on the bottom of the ocean. A White Star liner. No, not *that* White Star liner. This one you've probably never heard of. Unlike her more famous fleet mate, RMS *Republic* sank with relatively small loss of life. Three people died aboard her when she collided with another passenger ship off the coast of Nantucket in 1909. Over fifteen-hundred souls were lost on *Titanic* just three years later. The tragedy of *Titanic*, understandably so, greatly overshadows the *Republic* story. And yet the story of *Republic* is not without its own share of intrigue. Almost immediately upon *Republic*'s sinking came rumors, rumors of a lost treasure that was aboard her. A treasure of over $3 million in gold coins, a treasure that today, may be worth well over a billion dollars.

That treasure has been found. And the rumors have been

confirmed. Or maybe, more accurately, the rumors have been confirmed and therefore the treasure has been found. The confirmation of the rumors is the end result of years and years of investigation. I share the results of that investigation (most of the results anyway) with you here, within the pages of this book. As for the treasure itself, its precise location is now known. But reaching that location is not without its challenges. The treasure lies within the wreckage of the ship, 40 fathoms below the surface of the sea, all but out of reach without the aid of significantly expensive diving and salvage equipment. Several years ago, I dove down to the wreckage. At the time, however, I had no practical knowledge of where, precisely, to look for the treasure. Nor did I, at that time, have the knowledge to substantiate the rumors. I was looking, that is to say, for a treasure I didn't know for certain existed, in the midst of a sprawling field of wreckage where I didn't know where to look.

The things I didn't know then, I know now. What I had then, however; namely, the necessary salvage funds, I don't have now. But I soon will. And I will dive *Republic* again.

Until then, I welcome you to learn what I have learned, and how I came by the knowledge. For this is perhaps more than just the story of lost and found treasure. It is the story of a lost and found treasure hunter – off-course at times, frustrated beyond hope at times, despondent and ready to quit at times. But always something would come along to keep me in the hunt. And now, standing in the doorway of destiny, 40 fathoms away from the story's conclusion, it seems the appropriate time to reveal the secrets that I have discovered.

Take the information herein as you wish: evidence of certain treasure, or a tall tale of wishful thinking. Evidence of a hundred-year-old conspiracy of silence (there's a reason you've probably never heard of *Republic*), or an imaginative yarn. I trust you'll be entertained either way. But I challenge you to look closely at the evidence that I've spent my adult life accumulating. I believe there's more than enough of it. The ultimate answer, of course, one way or the other, lies deep beneath the sea. I'll get there, hopefully sooner rather than later.

Until then, I submit to you this.

~Captain Martin Bayerle

PROLOGUE

In the engine room of the luxury liner RMS *Republic*, with 742 passengers and crew aboard, oiler John Hart heard the order for "full speed ahead." It had come less than a minute after "full speed astern," which had come less than a minute after "stop." He would have little time to wonder at the seemingly conflicting orders from the bridge where Captain Inman Sealby had been busy dealing with the perilous effects of a thick morning fog that had enveloped his ship as she steamed just off the coast of Nantucket. Sealby had, at least according to White Star Line, owner of the ship, ordered *Republic*'s speed reduced and had signaled her presence by whistle at regular intervals. Neither effort, if indeed employed, would be enough to avert disaster.

At 5:40 a.m. on the morning of January 23rd, 1909, just seconds after John Hart heard "full speed ahead," the stem of the Lloyd Italiano liner S.S. *Florida* crashed through the bulkhead of

Republic, through inner and outer steel plates, forcing its way to within fifteen feet of where a stunned Hart was standing in the engine room. Reported Hart afterwards, "The vessel tore away everything on that side for twenty feet aft and then disappeared, and we could see the water rushing in below."

Sealby's desperate attempts at evading the *Florida* as she loomed out of the fog were futile. He'd ordered *Republic* hard over and ahead but the *Florida* hit her amidships on the port side at close to a right angle. Killed instantly in their cabins were Mary Lynch, wife of a prominent liquor businessman (who was critically injured himself and would die three days later) and banker W.J. Mooney. A shoe belonging to Mrs. Lynch was reported by Hart to have been "cut in two as if by a sharp axe." Three crewmen in the bow of the *Florida* were also killed.

Though she was cut down to below the waterline and taking on water, Sealby initially believed the *Republic* may well float indefinitely. She was a White Star liner, after all. A palatial steamer. With a series of watertight compartments, she was deemed "practically unsinkable." The words would echo a mere three years later as another "practically unsinkable" White Star liner would meet her demise in the North Atlantic at the hands of an iceberg.

Like *Titanic* after her, *Republic*, also built in Belfast at the Harland and Wolff shipyards, was modern, luxurious, and big. She was a steel, twin-screw, four-masted steamer of 15,378 gross tonnage. Five hundred seventy feet long, she had five decks and twelve watertight compartments. And, like *Titanic* after her, she would be lost to the sea.

In the radio room within minutes of the collision, Jack Binns, the ship's trained operator of the new Marconi wireless telegraph system, issued a C.Q.D. distress signal (the precursor to the S.O.S.), the first real practical use of the distress signal for such a major event. The system proved itself as the U.S. Coast Guard cutters *Gresham* and *Seneca* picked up the C.Q.D. and responded, along with half a dozen other ships. Meanwhile *Florida*, wounded but still under power and in no danger of foundering, came about and made herself available for the transfer of passengers from *Republic*. Though she might escape sinking, *Republic* was adrift and completely without power, a sitting duck in the fog of the busy shipping lane.

Florida, with close to a thousand passengers herself, took on *Republic*'s passengers, becoming dangerously overcrowded in the process. Ultimately, the passengers would be transferred again, to another White Star liner, *Baltic*, which had arrived some twelve hours after the collision, finding the *Republic* still afloat. *Baltic* had also received Binns's C.Q.D. It took 83 boatloads and 10 hours to complete the second transfer to *Baltic* and the open ocean rescue still stands as the largest on record.[1]

---

[1] In 2012, the *Costa Concordia* hit a reef off Isola del Giglio during an unofficial near-shore salute to the local islanders. Approximately 4,200 passengers and crew were taken ashore from the ship by lifeboats and helicopters or swam to the island. The *Costa Concordia* still remains above the waves at the time of this

Captain Sealby remained on his ship with a skeleton crew of volunteers as *Gresham* and *Seneca* began towing *Republic* toward New York in the hope of saving her. Meanwhile, the salvage tug *City of Everett* arrived on the scene, offering to pump out *Republic's* engine room and transport her cargo and passenger baggage back to New York on an accompanying barge. Sealby declined the offer and the towing continued. At first, it seemed *Republic* might make it. At worst, perhaps she could be towed into shallow water. But progress was slow through choppy seas and eventually it became clear that, although her watertight compartments had slowed the inevitable, the battle to save *Republic* would be lost. Jack Binns and the rest of the remaining crew were ordered off the ship by Sealby who stayed behind with the second officer. The two would ultimately be rescued from the water and at 8:07 p.m., Sunday, January 24, 1909, RMS *Republic* disappeared stern first into the dark waters of the Atlantic Ocean.

Save the three unfortunate passengers from *Republic* and the three unfortunate crew members from *Florida*, over 1,600 people were brought ashore safely. But almost immediately, rumors began to circulate that much more was lost than the six lives and ship herself. *The New York American* printed the following day that "an unconfirmed report has it a large sum of money was on board the *Republic* for the Italian earthquake sufferers [a December, 1908

---

writing, awaiting salvage removal.

earthquake in the Sicilian city of Messina had killed over 100,000 people], which may be one of the reasons the captain of *Republic* remained on his ship." Other reports referenced the loss of a sizeable Navy payroll as the *Republic* was to eventually steam to Gibraltar where President Teddy Roosevelt's "Great White Fleet" would be arriving as part of its famous around-the-world tour.

And still another rumor: three million dollars worth of American Eagle gold coins (worth somewhere over one billion dollars today). There was no easily attributable source of this rumor, no readily identifiable owner of the purported gold, and no clear reason for gold coins in such quantity to even be aboard. And yet the rumor persisted. A strange circumstance: no public inquiry into the sinking was ever held, an inquiry that would certainly have shed light on *Republic*'s lost cargoes. There were other strange circumstances and the rumor grew, as rumors may, over the course of a century, into legend. But sometimes, there's a grain of truth to rumors and once in a great while, a legend is revealed to be more than myth.

Secrets, as it turns out, don't always stay secret.

CHAPTER ONE

The Siren's Song

"To the Sirens first shalt thou come, who bewitch all men..."

— Homer

Life was good.

I was single, 28, owner of a dive shop, living in my dream home on Martha's Vineyard (just down the road, as it happened, from Carly Simon's nightclub, Hot Tin Roof), and sitting with a couple hundred grand in the bank. My unofficial occupation: treasure hunter.

A year earlier I'd accepted a settlement of an anti-trust suit I'd brought against certain members of the underwater diving industry who had illegally banded together to kill off my successful mail order equipment business. Working out of a dive shop in Brooklyn with a warehouse in Queens, I had been the answer to

the average diver's prayers, providing masks and fins and regu-
lators and wetsuits and all the requisite accessories at discounted
pricing, undercutting the standard 100% markup that all the dive
shops were getting from their customers. It was a business model
ahead of its time and it annoyed the hell out of the shops that, in
turn, demanded help from the manufacturers who, in turn, made
sure my ads wouldn't run in the popular trade magazines.

With the settlement money, I had a couple choices. I briefly
considered buying a resort in the Caribbean, some place where I
could run dive charters, sell equipment, teach SCUBA diving to
wealthy New York tourists in the winter. I flew down to look at a
place on St. Eustatius in the West Indies, but ultimately rejected
the idea of buying it. The resort didn't have everything I wanted;
it was on the wrong side of the island for one thing, facing the
rougher waters of the Atlantic rather than the calmer waters of
the Caribbean. But there was something else, too. Something back
in New England that I couldn't stop thinking about. Something I
couldn't leave behind.

With my dive shop and mail order business in New York
I had become well versed in the many shipwrecks that dotted the
Atlantic depths from Long Island up past Cape Cod and beyond.
There's really nothing else to dive there, after all. No colorful reefs
with schools of tropical fish. Just wrecks. Ships that had gone
down in storms, in fog, in battle. Schooners and freighters and
tugs and steamers. The locations of most had been identified and

plotted and you could find them using any decent navigational chart. But some were more elusive. There was one in particular: a huge passenger ship that went down in 1909. Though her location could only be guessed, it was her presumed depth that had kept her hidden away for so long. At over 250 feet below the surface, the RMS *Republic* was considered a "Triple D" threat: deep, dark, and dangerous.

But there were those rumors: gold, with a potential worth of well over a billion dollars. I knew *Republic* was out there somewhere, just waiting to be found. It was the Siren's song and I didn't stand a chance against her. I put the Caribbean resort idea on the back burner. Maybe someday. Maybe after my ship comes in, I thought. Or, more precisely, maybe after I go get her.

On Martha's Vineyard I set up a base of operations, met interesting people like Dan Aykroyd and John Belushi and James Taylor and others, some of whom became investors in my project. I got to know the diving community, too. It's not a big one. You learn quickly who has the right skills and equipment. I discovered that you learn too late whom you can trust.

Steve Bielenda was known as the "King of the Deep." His son Lance used to work for me in my shop in Brooklyn and I got to know them both well. Steve had a lot of experience running dive trips to the *Andrea Doria* which, it turned out, was lying just six miles from where we would ultimately find *Republic*. Steve, I thought, with his research vessel the *Wahoo* and his experienced

11

crew, was the right guy for the job. I approached him with my idea and we struck a deal for a five-day charter in early August of 1981.

I knew we might need most of those five days just to find *Republic*, let alone dive her. There was a lot of misinformation as to exactly where she was. There were conflicting reports from the very ships that tried to tow her in and there was even an additional location, the "official" location, given by the British Hydrographic Office. It wouldn't be until much later that I'd discern the reason for the misinformation. It wasn't accidental.

I invested in a Wesmar Side Scan sonar, an expensive but necessary device that would produce images for us of the sea floor, and I hired three skilled divers. Steve brought four divers along himself, so, with me included, we had eight guys ready to make what I had hoped would be the discovery of a lifetime.

The search on day one proved fruitless. We cruised to the official location and found exactly nothing. That night I took a hard look at the other two locations and did some interpolation. Using the Wesmar we undertook a slow grid search for the next day and a half, from one location to the other, and finally came across something. Something big. Steve killed the engines and we drifted slowly above the silhouette that had appeared on the scanner. The water was uncharacteristically flat that day and as we looked out across it, we could see intermittent spirals of oil breaking the glassy surface. *Republic* was coal-fired, of course, but

I knew she had tanks of machine oil and perhaps, just maybe, one of those had very recently rusted through. Whatever was below us, *Republic* or some other ship lost to the sea, she seemed to be beckoning to me with each rising bead of oil.

We dove in pairs, with two of Steve's divers going down first, including Janet Bieser, an experienced diver who had dived the *Andrea Doria*. Sending the captain's crew first is standard operational procedure; the captain's crew goes down and secures a grappling hook to the wreck ("setting the hook," as it's called). With the depth, we could do no more than 20 minutes at the bottom, and even that would require one-and-a-half to two hours of decompression. For safety, we staggered the dives in half-hour intervals, overlapping them to ensure that two divers were going down as two were coming up, just in case there was a problem with someone's ascent. The drawback, though, was that the team going down couldn't talk to the team coming up. You didn't know what they'd found. Nobody could compare notes until we were all back on the *Wahoo*.

My first team didn't make it beyond 185 feet. That kind of depth can do funny things to you. Decompression sickness, oxygen toxicity, nitrogen narcosis – lots of scary things can happen. Not to mention just the unsettling feeling of being so deep, having so much water over your head. And the darkness. It can be disturbing. And these guys still had 75 feet to go. They quit and came back up. When my turn came, I managed to make it all the way down, even though I'd never before been below 130 feet.

At around 230 feet I found myself looking at a gargantuan, rusted metal wall of some description, but that's about all I could make out. Whatever was down there was immense. But it was like lying next to an elephant, seeing just a tiny piece of it and trying to determine what it is. And I started feeling the effects of nitrogen narcosis, a dangerous intoxicating feeling that comes as a result of breathing air at depth. It makes you think you can do things you can't do, frequently causing you to cease caring about your own personal safety. The effects are often cited in dive classes under a rule referred to as Martini's Law, which essentially says that breathing nitrogen as a part of compressed air produces an effect roughly equivalent to having one dry martini on an empty stomach for every fifty feet of descent. It affects most divers at between 100 and 150 feet, and of course we had gone far below that. I felt suddenly tempted to take off and just start swimming haphazardly around the wreck, but my experience kicked in and I recognized the feeling for what it was. I stuck to the mantra: plan your dive and dive your plan. But fifteen minutes sure went by fast.

I had a bottle of champagne aboard the *Wahoo* that I had planned on opening in celebration of finding *Republic*, but none of us could (or would) say for certain what we'd seen that afternoon. I put the bottle away and hoped we'd have better luck the next day, maybe find something that would prove her identity. But then Steve cut the expedition short, saying something about needing to go in and prepare for his next charter. Something didn't seem quite right to me about Steve's excuse. We had an understanding, a contract. I had another day of the *Wahoo* and her crew coming to me. But I didn't say a word. It was Steve's vessel. He was the captain. We docked and I wrote him a check and got my gear off the boat and thanked him. Then I went home and called my bank and stopped the check.

My sense about Steve cutting things short was right on the money. I would come to learn years later that Janet had taken a photograph of the wreck while she was down, a shot of the bow. They'd been able to identify the ship. It was, in fact, *Republic*. It was my charter. It was my expedition, research, and equipment. The problem was, Steve wanted to take credit for the find.

I eventually settled with Steve on a breach of contract suit and although I've seen a few sources here and there that erroneously credit Steve with the find, he never really did anything with the knowledge other than run a few charters to the wreck. Inevitably word leaked out about *Republic*'s location and when I got a phone call several months later from my dive shop landlord and fellow diver Barry Clifford, I knew I needed to do something to protect my rights. Barry, catching the treasure-hunting bug from me, would take credit for discovering the wreck of the *Whydah*, a pirate ship sunk in a storm off Cape Cod way back in 1717. Over the phone that day I could tell Barry was trying to pump me for information about *Republic*, telling me he knew the coordinates, reading them off to me, hoping, I could guess, that I'd confirm them. I said it was good talking with him and then called my attorney and we filed a maritime claim for an "unidentified wreck and abandoned steam vessel." (We actually ended up using Barry's *Whydah* claim as a template.) I didn't know about Janet's photograph at the time, so I still didn't know what we'd found.

Treasure hunting, as it turns out, is about 5% seeking treasure and about 95% fighting for your legal rights to it. In late summer of '82, a company called Underwater Completion Team came along from New Iberia, Louisiana. The owner, Cuz Daugherty, a colorful Cajun character, had gotten wind of my "unidentified wreck" from Kent Guernsey, one of my own divers who had gone to work for Cuz. Kent told Cuz he ought to contact me, maybe help me identify the ship we'd found. Cuz's company was one of the many that had been doing underwater work for the oil companies, but when the economy turned they found themselves looking for other ways to make a profit – even hunting for underwater treasure. Cuz and I talked by phone about the idea of his company coming up and doing some survey work on the wreck.

Cuz came up, all right, but not just to see me. After a brief search for the *Central America*, Cuz took his boat and did a bandit dive on *Republic*. Kent told me about Cuz's dive, more loyal to me than his new employer. I had to sue Cuz, but what he brought up from the wreck – artifacts like dinner plates with the famous White Star insignia – at least made it possible to positively identify

16

the sunken ship as *Republic*.

In June of '83, now with positive identification, I made another trip to the site, this time with a U.S. marshal. We "arrested" the vessel, a preliminary legal step towards obtaining prime salvage rights. But a legal challenge would come just three months later. James Amplas of Northern Ocean Services from Orlando came out of the blue, making a court case that he'd been preparing salvage operations for *Republic* for the past four years. The problem was, he hadn't bothered to tell anyone about it until he came across my legal claim. We secured a temporary restraining order followed by an injunction. By November, the U.S. District Court in Boston officially granted salvage rights to me, the Honorable Judge Walter J. Skinner making the decision. It wouldn't be the last time I'd find myself in front of Judge Skinner.[2]

Now that I'd obtained salvage rights, it was time to move things forward. My next expedition had to count. I needed a ship with pressurized chambers that would allow saturation diving, a technology that allows a diver to stay down for hours at a time. And I would need that ship for months, to fully explore the whole site. And a skilled crew. And I would need the plans of *Republic*, not the schematics that the passengers were given so they could

---

[2] Judge Skinner's real claim to fame would be presiding over a certain trial involving a lawsuit against a large corporation for environmental contamination, contamination that resulted in several cases of leukemia. The case was dramatized in the film *A Civil Action*, starring John Travolta. John Lithgow played the part of Skinner and he played it well.

make their way around the ship, but the actual detailed drawings that showed where storage and baggage compartments were and nooks and crannies that only the crew could access. All of this meant that I needed investors. And that meant something else; I needed to do my homework. I needed to make sure the rumors were true.

I'd been doing some research on *Republic* for several years, but now I stepped it up. In a sense, I had done things backwards in 1981. I'd had a lot of money and so I just went ahead and tried to carry out a salvage operation. On a ship that had nothing on board her, so far as I could prove. The historical artifacts we could have brought to the surface might have been interesting, maybe worth a spot in a maritime museum somewhere, but not enough to warrant an expedition costing hundreds of thousands of dollars, potentially even millions – much more money than I had. My interest had been based on rumors. Now I needed to determine if the rumors were true.

The research was lengthy and painstaking. I dug through newspaper accounts and sifted through public records and chased money trails and did transaction analysis and analyzed import/export data from the 1909 New York gold market. In fact, I researched the gold market from 1904 through 1914, educating myself on the how, why, who, what, and where of the market. I followed every possible, probable, and even improbable lead I could unearth, from New York to Belfast to London to Paris.

My goal was to find the truth. I needed to know. It became all-consuming. It was the Siren's song. If the rumors weren't true, if the story of gold was a canard, well, then there would always be that Caribbean resort idea. If the rumors were true, however, then I'd need to prove their veracity in order to attract the investment money I'd need. I'd have to establish unequivocally that there would be $3 million in 1909 gold aboard *Republic*. Or, failing that, I'd need to prove the converse, if only for my own satisfaction. I'd have to do the logically impossible and prove a negative – that *Republic* had no gold aboard, or at least not enough to justify salvage. Not enough juice to make the squeeze worthwhile. If I couldn't prove that, then there would always be the possibility in my mind that the gold was down there. The Siren's call would continue to haunt me.

"Follow the money," Deep Throat advised Woodward and Bernstein. The questions, it seemed to me, most in need of answering were these: Whose $3 million would have been aboard *Republic*? Where was it headed? And why was it shrouded in such secrecy?

What I initially uncovered was fascinating, and more than sufficient to attract the investors I needed. We did a full-scale salvage in 1987. More about that later; for the moment, let's just say it wasn't completely successful. But then I went even deeper into the research. There's research, and then there's pit bull research. I grabbed on and wouldn't let go. And I uncovered some additional things. Things that went beyond fascinating. Things that were jaw-dropping. Things I'd wished I'd known before that 1987 expedition.

But I know them now. I have a bas-relief of Teddy Roosevelt above my desk and often I look upon it and say, *I know, Mr. President. I know what you knew.*

And so it only remained to get back down to *Republic*. But sometimes life doesn't always go as planned. The gods laugh at the plans of men, goes the saying, and for me they must have been rolling. For the moment, let's just say I got a little sidetracked. There would be hurdles and legal challenges. There would be a marriage and a divorce. There would be hardships and privation. I would go on to lose everything: my home, my family, my legal career, my liberty. You know, life got in the way. And it would all play out in slow motion as years went by. The treasure would have to wait.

But at least I had the research.

CHAPTER TWO

The Ship

"A 'Palatial' Steamer. The new twin-screw steamer 'Republic,' 15,400 tons ... will stand comparison with anything afloat for the excellence, comliness, and comfort of passenger accommodation. The 'Republic' is a vessel which calls for distinct mention among many notable craft."

— White Star Line booklet, circa 1908

In 1903, Theodore Roosevelt was busy filling, maybe overfilling, the office of President of the United States, having been installed as such two years earlier upon the assassination of William McKinley. The "big stick" president had been a war hero, charging up San Juan Hill with his Rough Riders back in '98, a decisive battle in the Spanish-American War. "A splendid little war," the future president had called it. At the time of the war he was Assistant Secretary of the Navy, a position he resigned in order to fight; assistant secretaries don't charge up hills. But before he did so, he managed to propel the United States Navy toward readiness and worldwide respect. A student of naval history, Roosevelt would show off his Navy in earnest as President, sending sixteen battleships – "the Great White Fleet" – around the world between 1907 and 1909.

In 1903, the southern tip of Italy – the toe of the boot, the area known as Calabria – was a quiet, agricultural region loaded with quaint little villages and olive trees, basking in the Mediterranean sun. Off the coast, straight out from Villa San Giovanni, were the island of Sicily and the town, and province, of Messina, also largely agricultural. Also beautiful. Five years later, as 1908 would come to a close, the deadliest earthquake in European history would shake the ground directly under Messina for almost a full minute, creating, within moments, a devastating tsunami. Ninety percent of Messina would be destroyed and at least 100,000 people would be killed in the Messina and Calabria regions, 200,000 left homeless. The world community would respond with massive relief efforts in January of 1909.

In 1903, in early February, Tsar Nicholas II of Russia was hosting a luxurious ball in his great Winter Palace in St. Petersburg. Guests were dressed in 17th century fashion, from the days of the early Romanov dynasty. It was a spectacular ball, and the last real celebration of the crumbling dynasty of a crumbling nation. A year later, Mother Russia would be at war with the empire of Japan. Both nations had designs on Manchuria and

Korea – Japan, becoming a modern nation, looking to expand her interests beyond the shores of her crowded islands, Russia seeking a warm water port and a buffer zone to her south.

The war would prove costly for Nicholas, politically and financially. Russia would be handed a stunning defeat by the Japanese. The Tsar, already losing popularity due to his country's rapidly-deteriorating economic conditions, would bear witness to even greater unrest and discontent; fourteen years after that magnificent 1903 ball in the Winter Palace would come the inevitable Russian Revolution. In immediate financial terms, the war left Russia on the hook for $160 million – a loan to fight the Japanese from the French. It would be a five-year note, due and payable in May of 1909.

In 1903, the White Star Line was barely beginning its heyday of providing luxurious passenger experiences for those crossing the Atlantic Ocean between Europe and the United States. Just four years earlier, White Star launched *Oceanic*, the largest steamship ever built up until that time (supplanted in 1901 by another White Star ship, the *Celtic*). Known as the Queen of the Ocean, she was over 17,000 gross tons and built to accommodate 2,000 people, passengers and crew. *Oceanic* would be followed quickly by *Celtic*, *Cedric*, *Baltic*, and *Adriatic*. Eventually would come *Olympic*, *Britannic*, and *Titanic*. All of White Star's liners, at least up until World War I, were built in Belfast by shipbuilders Harland and Wolff.

In 1903, Harland and Wolff built the S.S. *Columbus* for the Dominion Line, a sister company of White Star, both owned by the International Mercantile Marine Company, a conglomerate of shipping companies put together by wealthy financier J.P. Morgan with the idea of monopolizing the transatlantic shipping business. *Columbus* sailed two voyages with Dominion, placed in service between Liverpool (via nearby Queenstown) and Boston and making her first transatlantic crossing on October 1st, 1903. For several years she held the record for the fastest passage between Queenstown and Boston. In 1904, she was sold to White Star and, in keeping with their fleet names ending in "ic", was rechristened RMS *Republic*.

Republic was a steel, twin-screw, four-masted vessel, at 15,378 gross tons, 14,301 under deck, 9,742 net registered tonnage, and her displacement on a mean draft of 34 feet was 27,220 tons. Her length was 570 feet, her breadth was 67-foot, 8-inches, and she ran 24 feet in depth. She had five decks, 12 watertight compartments, and was equipped with electric light and refrigeration machinery. She had accommodations for 280 first-class passengers, 250 in her second cabin, and 2,300 in steerage. She had a crew of about 300. She could cruise at a top speed of 16 knots.

Republic was one of the most modern, most luxurious passenger vessels afloat. Soon after White Star acquired her, she went into their Mediterranean service, sailing out of Boston to Naples and Genoa, and then eventually sailing out of New York.

Newspaper and magazine advertisements trumpeted the "fast, twin-screw passenger steamer" scheduled from New York "via Azores to Gibraltar, Algiers, Naples, Genoa and Alexandria." Because of the number of rich and famous Americans who traveled by her, she became known as the "Millionaires' Ship."[3]

She boasted an opulent dining saloon with a stained glass dome, polished hardwood wainscoting, and a seating capacity of 200. She had a well-stocked library for those, according to White Star's literature, "who are on the outlook for a contemplative nook, where the mind can roam over the world at large, and commune with the spirits of the great departed." *Republic* had a well-appointed smoking room where (the same White Star literature), "many congregate to enjoy the fragrant Havana, or some favorite brand in the briar bowl," and, on her Promenade Deck, a lounge that was "by general consent regarded as peculiarly the domain of the ladies." Throughout the ship the upholstery was plush. First-class cabins were richly furnished.

It was all a part of White Star's commitment to passenger comfort. *Republic* was fast, and that was a major selling point for transatlantic passengers, but above all else she was comfortable – and safe. That was another major selling point. The deluxe furnishings added to the secure, staid feel that White Star was intent on presenting.

---

[3] *Daily Telegraph of London*, "The Republic and The Dehli", April 16, 1912 (In regard to the loss of RMS *Titanic*.)

While the comfort and luxuriousness of *Republic* was something a wealthy, first-class passenger might well expect, what made White Star's approach different from, say, the approach of the Cunard Steamship Company, Ltd. (White Star's chief rival), was White Star's expansion of her comforts to those in second class and even steerage. Though a passenger in steerage couldn't expect a cabin comparable to a first-class passenger's (in fact steerage was typically managed dormitory style), he or she could at least expect comfortable, clean accommodations with some modicum of privacy. Food was decent and second and third classes even had their own dining saloons, with "less of the finer artistic effects than 1st class," said the literature, "but still (holding) the attractiveness of the ship's overall beauty." Each class had its own smoking room as well.

With this unique approach, White Star was well positioned to take advantage of the huge emigrant traffic. Nine million people made their way to the shores of the United States in the decade that began the 20th century, many at that time from Ireland and the U.K., but many more beginning to come from Italy as well as the Slavic regions controlled by the slowly dying Austro-Hungarian Empire. Hence, the Mediterranean route. It provided a tourist destination for wealthy Americans on the way there, and a means of coming to America for thousands wanting to leave Europe on the way back.

Although White Star may have been profitable, the

holding company, International Mercantile Marine Company, was not. This was a rare thing for any endeavor put together by John Pierpont Morgan. Among other successes as investor and financier, Morgan created Chase Manhattan Bank; merged Federal Steel, a company he created, with several other steel companies including Andrew Carnegie's to form U.S. Steel; and turned Thomas Edison's electric company into General Electric.

Morgan's idea of merging the transatlantic shipping businesses was an unusual defeat for him. But I.M.M. faced difficulties with anti-trust legislation and, as well, had to compete against Cunard, which was being subsidized by the British government.

And then would come April of 1912. The company would suffer a devastating loss through its White Star Line. The largest passenger ship in the world at the time would sink on her maiden voyage with the loss of 1,517 people. *Titanic* was covered, mostly, by Lloyds and by I.M.M.'s own self-insurance fund, but the blow to White Star's esteem coupled with I.M.M.'s overleveraging and undercapitalization would eventually lead I.M.M. to bankruptcy in 1915.

The huge loss of life, the fact that it was the largest passenger steamer afloat, the fact that it was on its very first voyage, all came together to turn the story of *Titanic* into legend. The practically unsinkable portrayal (she was never actually advertised as "unsinkable" without the qualifier contrary to myth) added to the legend with its deadly irony.

But *Republic* was considered practically unsinkable as well, three years prior. The watertight compartment idea of both ships was played up as a failsafe way of confining a watery breach to a single, small section, thus keeping the rest of the ship dry and safe. Though the word "unsinkable" never appeared on *Republic's* literature, it's clear that was the impression that White Star, indeed all of the passenger ship lines under I.M.M., wanted to convey. Richards Mills and Company, managers of the Dominion Line, wrote about the safety of their ships in a 1901 marketing booklet entitled "The Mediterranean Illustrated":

> The safety of the Dominion Line ships has been careful-
> ly looked after in every point. They all have double bot-
> toms and many bulkheads by which the ship is divided
> into watertight compartments. These would positively
> prevent serious results in case of collision, as by them
> the water which might get into the ship is restricted to
> the one compartment injured – and even if several of
> these should be filled the boat could still proceed.

The impression stuck. When *Republic* went down, all the papers reported on the irony. The January 23rd, 1909 *New York Evening Sun* talked about the "elaborate watertight compartment system." She was, reported the *Sun*, "...as nearly unsinkable in theory as a vessel could be made when she was designed." From the January 24th *New York American*: "As nearly unsinkable as a vessel could be made." From the *New York Herald* of the same day:

"In theory, at least, the ship was constructed so as to prove unsinkable." From *The Scientific American* on February 6th: "When she started from New York on her fatal trip, she was considered to be practically unsinkable by collision."

If the "practically unsinkable" impression stuck, the lesson learned from *Republic* did not. *Titanic* boasted the safety of her watertight compartments as well and the public still bought into it, notwithstanding *Republic*'s direct evidence that, as Walter Lord perhaps put it best in his famous book about *Titanic, A Night to Remember,* "the appearance of safety was mistaken for safety itself."[4] Although good in theory, the watertight compartment concept was no match for a gash the length of what an iceberg produced in the side of *Titanic.*

The truth of the matter for *Titanic* would be that the risk of a catastrophe was most likely aided and abetted by White Star Line itself. Speed was a crucial factor. It wasn't enough to supply safety and security and comfort (and luxury, at least for first-class passengers); it was competitively important for White Star to provide its passengers with a transatlantic crossing that was swift and reliable. It was important that she be kept on schedule. Cunard proudly boasted its fast ships; *Mauretania* and *Lusitania,* both launched in 1907, provided Cunard with passenger vessels that could steam at 24 knots, while *Titanic* cruised at 21 knots (*Republic*

---

[4] Longmans, Green and Co.; First English edition (1956).

just 16). Additionally, mail had to be kept on time. R.M.S stood for Royal Mail Ship, after all; being under contract to the British Royal Mail service provided White Star with a significant portion of its revenue.

In fact, speed was a risk assumed by the whole passenger ship industry, a practice that didn't end even with *Titanic's* demise. The P&O liner *Egypt* went down in the English Channel in 1922, the result of a collision in fog. She reportedly reduced her speed but that wasn't necessarily the norm. "It is well known," noted David Scott in *The Egypt's Gold*, "that liners, especially mailboats, are often obliged to steam fast in fog to keep up on their time-tables."[5]

Thirteen years before *Egypt*, the ship steaming through fog was *Republic*. Her captain was Inman Sealby. Sealby, born in England in 1862, immigrated to America with his family when he was just a boy. While still in his teens he became an apprentice with the very ship line that would ultimately make him a captain. That was not a coincidence. His father Joseph moved the family to New Jersey so that he could open up what would be the American branch of White Star in Jersey City. (Later he would buy a second home in Vineland, New Jersey, where Inman would spend most of his childhood.) Joseph's uncle was none other than Thomas Henry Ismay.

---

[5] Penguin Books, 1939, p. 268.

It was Thomas Henry Ismay who bought the White Star company in 1868, pulling it out of bankruptcy. Thomas's son would go on to rather infamous renown aboard *Titanic*. J. Bruce Ismay succeeded his father as chairman of White Star upon his father's death in 1899, overseeing the sale of the company to I.M.M. and then becoming president of I.M.M. in 1904. Eight years later, he was aboard *Titanic* on April 14th, 1912, reportedly ordering Captain Edward J. Smith to pick up *Titanic*'s speed in an effort to arrive in New York ahead of schedule, thereby contributing (if not downright causing) the fatal collision.[6] When the ship sank, he grabbed a spot in a lifeboat, eschewing the famous "women and children first" dictate. It should be noted that the veracity of both charges remains controversial to this day. Ismay denied he spoke to the captain about *Titanic*'s speed and claimed that he boarded a lifeboat only after observing that there were no more women and children in the lifeboat's vicinity.

Meanwhile, J. Bruce Ismay's first cousin once removed, Inman Sealby, did four years apprenticeship and served on a series of White Star ships, rising quickly in the ranks and becoming, at 33, the youngest captain in White Star's fleet, taking command of *Coptic* out of San Francisco in 1895. Until *Republic*, his biggest claim to fame was being commander of the ship that, in July of 1898, brought the news to Honolulu that Hawaii was to be

---

[6] The claim was specifically rejected by the British Board of Trade's public inquiry concerning the *Titanic* disaster.

annexed by the United States. It was joyous news to the islands whose residents presented Sealby with a silver cup bearing the inscription: "Annexation. Presented by citizens to Captain Inman Sealby who brought the good news to Honolulu."

Fame for Sealby, unwanted fame, would come again eleven years later, commanding the RMS *Republic*.

CHAPTER THREE

Collision

"Who did that?!"

— Unknown passenger at John Ward's poker table

An article in the February 4th, 1909 edition of *The Eastern Underwriter* reported that a woman making her very first trip across the Atlantic, aboard the White Star liner RMS *Republic*, had had a dreadful premonition, one she just couldn't seem to shake. The woman had become convinced something terrible was going to befall her on her pending voyage. It didn't help that she knew *Republic* was departing on a Friday, a day, superstition says, on which it is bad luck to set sail. So strong was the premonition that the woman, bound for a Roman holiday with her husband, a respected Boston businessman, insisted on taking out a special accident insurance policy before the two embarked. Mary Lynch's purchase of the $10,000 policy came over husband Eugene's objections.

In addition to their plans for Rome, Eugene was intent on taking a little side trip with a friend, journalist James B. Connolly, also booked on the *Republic*. The two wanted to see Sicily, site of a recent earthquake. On December 28th, 1908, a magnitude 7.2 quake had decimated the city of Messina, destroying ninety percent of the buildings and killing over 70,000 people. The resulting tsunami claimed more than 30,000 additional lives in the Italian region of Calabria. Connolly was being sent by the *New York Herald* to cover the relief efforts. The *Republic*, in fact, had just returned from the area, arriving in New York on January 13th, 1909, carrying refugees from the disaster. Now she was heading back.

Although Eugene Lynch chafed at spending money on an unnecessary insurance policy for a voyage aboard a practically unsinkable ship, he apparently spared no expense on his and his wife's accommodations. He had booked a luxurious first-class stateroom on the ship's top saloon deck. Next door to the Lynches were the Mooneys, William James and Oakella, from North Dakota. W.J. Mooney was a successful banker, presumably looking forward to the warmth of southern Italy as a welcome respite from the cold North Dakota winter. Immediately below the Lynches' cabin was ten-year-old Hallie Davis, granddaughter of Henry G. Davis, a senator from West Virginia. Hallie, a precocious child by all accounts, was traveling with her mother, grandmother, and brother.[7]

Other interesting and notable first-class passengers aboard the "Millionaires' Ship" included James Ross Mellon, president of both Mellon Bank and the City Deposit Bank of Pittsburgh, traveling with his wife Rachel and their daughter; historian and author Alice Morse Earl; General Brayton Ives who had served in the Civil War, was former president of the New York Stock Exchange, former president of the Northern Pacific Railway, president of the Williamsburg Trust Company and Metropolitan Trust Company, and director of both the Westinghouse Electric and Manufacturing Company and the National Bank of Commerce, accompanied by his valet; Mrs. H. L. Griggs, wife of Herbert L. Griggs, president of the Bank of New York; Professor John M. Coulter, world-renowned author on the subject of botany and founder of the *Botanical Gazette* (today the *International Journal of Plant Sciences*); Samuel Cupples, an elderly St. Louis millionaire and philanthropist, along with his daughter Amelia and granddaughters Gladys, Maude, and Martha, and his personal physician, Dr. A.J. Wagers, all of them bound for an eight-month trip through Egypt and the Holy Land; Monsignor Paul Burchesi, Archbishop of Montreal; John W. Ward, treasurer of the Manhattan Opera House on his way to Europe for health reasons and who would bide his time on

---

[7] Sodi, Diana (Hallie's daughter), interview for *Rescue at Sea*, Dir. Ben Loeterman. Prod. Liz Carver, Nancy Fraser. 1999, A Ben Loeterman Productions, Inc. film for *The American Experience*. VHS.

board playing poker; and various and sundry millionaire businessmen and politicians as well as at least one count and countess.

There were a total of 250 passengers booked for first class accommodations, with fewer in steerage – 211, many of whom were Italians headed back to Sicily and south Italy to find parents and siblings and cousins who hadn't been heard from since the devastating earthquake. Most of the others in steerage, according to a *New York Sun* article from January 24th, 1909, "were Portuguese bound for the Azores and Madeira, with here and there a Slav rattling money in his pocket, who was returning home to be a great fellow in his own town while the money lasted."

There were no passengers in the second-class section of *Republic*.[8] Those who were ticketed for second class were moved to first. The reasons were vague, but of course no one complained. It was a curious point, but nothing anyone might have thought too much about at the time.

Two weeks before *Republic* was to set sail from New York, the S.S. *Florida*, a steamship owned by the Italian shipping company Lloyd Italiano, had left Naples for New York. Eight-hundred and fifty passengers were aboard her, many of whom were refugees from the earthquake, booked in steerage, some with little more in the way of possessions than the clothes on their backs. Steerage aboard *Florida* wasn't as comfortable as steerage on a

---

[8] *New York Sun,* January 24, 1909, p. 2:6.

White Star liner. Passengers were packed into tight quarters and slept on bunks stacked atop one another.

Commanding the *Florida* was 28-year-old Captain Angelo Ruspini on his second transatlantic crossing as captain of the ship. One of his crew members was 14-year-old Salvatore D'Amico, making his very first voyage, as much to escape as to take to the sea. Salvatore had lost his entire family in the earthquake and his home lay in ruins. There was nothing at all left for him in Sicily.[9]

Twelve days later, with *Florida* just a few hundred miles from New York, RMS *Republic* left New York Harbor. It was 3:00 p.m., January 22nd, 1909. A Friday.

Passengers enjoyed their dinners and the various amenities the ship had to offer as *Republic* made her way out of New York and along the coast of Long Island, headed for open water. Ten-year-old Hallie Davis wandered about the ship and stumbled upon a small cabin where a young officer named Jack Binns had been operating the new Marconi device – a wireless radio transmitter. He invited Hallie in and showed her how the wireless worked. John Ward found a poker game. James Connolly walked along the cold deck. Other passengers bided their time in the smoking room or the library. In time, most of the passengers turned in for the night. Connolly stayed above, looking out at the water.

James Connolly was a popular journalist and writer. His

---

[9] *New York Times,* January 26th, 1909, p.2.

accounts of the Spanish-American War, in which he served, had been published in the *Boston Globe*. Other journalistic pieces followed, as did his popular short stories and novels of the sea. An interesting claim to fame was his participation in the 1896 Olympic games, the first of the modern games, winning the initial event, the triple jump (then called the "hop, skip, and jump") and, by so doing, becoming the first Olympic champion since the days of ancient Greece. In addition to traveling aboard *Republic* to cover the earthquake aftermath for the *Herald*, Connolly was planning on meeting the U.S. Navy battleship fleet, finishing up its famous circumnavigation of the globe, in Gibraltar. A personal friend of Teddy Roosevelt, Connolly had been invited to sail back home aboard the USS *Vermont*.

As Connolly looked out over the water, Captain Inman Sealby was on the bridge, watching warily as a fog began to move in. Dense, and then denser. Connolly would later report the speed at which *Republic* was going in the fog made him nervous as he watched the black water below him speeding past. *Republic* was in a busy shipping channel, after all. Connolly eventually retired to his cabin and *Republic* continued on her way for several hours through the fog.

Ahead of *Republic*, Captain Angelo Ruspini's *Florida* had fallen victim to the same disorienting fog. His ship was 30 miles off course. Sealby heard *Florida*'s fog horn in the distance and re-plied in kind. In the fog, Sealby couldn't tell how far away *Florida* was, or from which direction she was coming, but the horn blasts were getting closer. He ordered two successive blasts, thus signaling he would be turning his ship to port and expecting the other ship to do the same; the ships would pass each other on their starboard sides.

What happened next is a matter of some conjecture. *Florida* might have mistakenly turned the wrong way, turned too late, or not turned at all. Oiler John Hart and greaser Thomas McInerney in *Republic*'s engine room would later report to the press an order for full speed ahead after an order for full speed astern after an order for a complete stop. Sealby, seeing *Florida* looming out of the fog, coming directly at him, might have tried all three in desperation. A full inquiry might have fleshed out an accurate chain of events, had there been a full inquiry.

Meanwhile, in the first-class smoking room, at approximately 5:40 a.m. on the morning of the 23rd, John Ward sat back in his overstuffed leather chair and looked at the cards in his hand: three jacks and two threes. An all-night poker game was wrapping up with one final hand to determine who would take a sixty-dollar pot. Ward had just bet the limit on his full house when a tremendous crash knocked the table over and sent the five players to the floor. One man jumped up, having drawn a pistol, screaming, "Who did that?!" Quickly it dawned on the group that the cause of the upturned table and chairs was surely external to the game and they all scampered topside to find out exactly what was transpiring.[10]

In the engine room, John Hart saw the bow of *Florida*, having torn a gaping hole in the side of *Republic*, come to rest just five yards from where he was standing. Hallie Davis awoke to a frightening jolt, causing her to leap out of her bed. Jack Binns, who had retired from his duties several hours earlier, was knocked out of his. All over the ship the passengers and crew were shaken by the impact. Dr. J. Arthur Lamb reported later that he assumed the ship had hit an iceberg, presaging the White Star sinking three years later.[11]

James Connolly rushed out of his cabin and up the ship's grand staircase to discover dozens of fellow passengers, all in various stages of dress, hurrying up to the deck to determine the cause of the impact. Jack Binns, quickly realizing the magnitude of the situation, headed directly for his Marconi room, only to find that three of the walls had been crushed in. Fortunately the wireless was still functional but before he could use it, water, flooding into the generator room below, rendered it powerless. Within minutes of the collision, *Republic* had gone completely dark. While stewards very calmly and efficiently hurried throughout the ship with candles and oil lamps, lighting the way for passengers groping their way along dark corridors, Binns went down below and retrieved portable batteries from which he could muster

---

[10] *New York World*, January 28, 1909, p. 3:3.

[11] *Washington Evening Star*, January 26th, 1909, p. 9:5.

enough power to get his Marconi working again. At 6:00 a.m., twenty minutes after the collision, Binns telegraphed a "C.Q.D.", C.Q. meaning attention all stations and D standing for distress. A C.Q.D. signal had been designated by the Marconi company as a general distress call just a few years earlier, replaced eventually by the clearer S.O.S., a simple three dots, in Morse code, followed by three dashes followed by three dots, then repeated.

As the passengers began congregating above, the crew kept them calm and stewards passed out hot coffee, whiskey upon request. John Ward and his poker-playing associates, still clutching their cards, compared hands and determined that Ward's full house was the winner, making a gentlemen's agreement to settle up later, the pot having been left below. Hallie Davis and her family made it up on deck, her mother and grandmother grabbing blankets and jewelry before fleeing the cabin. Samuel Cupples made it above with the help of his personal physician who had managed to grab Cupples's overcoat and shoes before abandoning their cabin, leaving an estimated $25,000 in family jewelry behind. Once the passengers were above, orders were given by the ship's officers that they could not return to their cabins.

The crew down below, meanwhile, were facing challenges of their own. In the engine room, John Hart, Thomas McInerney, and several others had managed to close five of the hand-screwed, watertight doors, but the length of the gash below the ship's waterline and the damage done (one of the engine room's bulkheads had been torn away) made it impossible for the pumps to keep up with the rate of water coming in. An even more immediate problem was that the water was headed for the boiler room, producing a possibility of explosion should the cold water make sudden impact with the hot boilers. The crew did what they could to quickly cool the boilers, raking the hot coals out of them, then made for the ladders to get out. One man, J. G. Lagg, stayed behind, wading through the rising water, to open the boiler's feed checks, allowing them to be flooded slowly, minimizing the risk of explosion. Then Lagg scrambled up the ladder as well, guided through the darkness up the 160 rungs, as were the others, by a few emergency oil lamps along the way.

As day began to break, the passengers and crew were able to get a better look at the damage done. James Connolly could see that several of the topside staterooms had been demolished, the worst being the one occupied by his friend Eugene Lynch and Eugene's wife Mary. *Republic* was beginning to slowly list. *Florida*, meanwhile, had receded back into the fog. On deck of *Republic*, Captain Sealby gave the order to abandon ship. The passengers were to be loaded into lifeboats "women and children first," an established protocol that would be made more famous three years later on the deck of *Titanic*. After the women and children, it would be first-class passengers and then the rest. The crew, of course, would be the last to leave.

Jack Binns came out of his wrecked wireless room, having

made contact with the Marconi land station at Siasconsett on Nantucket, to confer with his captain and then returned, delivering a message from Sealby that read, "*Republic* rammed by unknown steamer 175 miles east Ambrose Light[ship]. No danger to lives."

The crew, meanwhile, darting around the ship looking for passengers, came across Eugene Lynch, critically injured, the mangled body of his beloved Mary lying still just a few feet away. Next door, W.J. Mooney's decapitated body was also discovered. Their identities would be confirmed shortly afterwards when a passenger roll call was undertaken. Mary's premonition had come true.

Drifting nearby *Republic*, now visible to her passengers, was *Florida*, her bow twisted and crumpled in, but in no apparent danger of sinking. Captain Angelo Ruspini was dealing with his own problems. In stark contrast to the rather orderly manner of *Republic*'s passengers, Ruspini's complement was on the verge of panic. Just weeks before, most of those in steerage had experienced the deadly tremor of a cataclysmic earthquake. Now, on the lower decks of *Florida*, they had just experienced a thunderous jolt the likes of which must have seemed every bit as frightening. In time, *Florida*'s crew members were able to convince the passengers that the ship was in no further danger and calm was eventually restored.

A roll call was also taken on *Florida*. Three crew members

who had been asleep in the forecastle at the time of the collision were found dead, one of whom was Salvatore D'Amico, the 14-year-old cabin boy who had just lost everything to the earthquake.

CHAPTER FOUR

Lost

"Gallant ship and gallant crew,
Gallant Captain, here's a hail!
Tho the knightly days be fled,
Heroism is not dead;
Souls are valiant, hearts are true,
And the brave shall still prevail!"

— Clinton Scollard, "The Republic"

In addition to the Marconi land station on Nantucket, the C.Q.D. Jack Binns sent was received by a number of other ships in the area, including another White Star liner, *Baltic*, a Cunard liner, *Lucania*, the French liner *La Lorraine*, the Anchor Line vessel *Furnessia*, the U.S. Navy torpedo boat *Cushing*, and the U.S. Revenue Cutters *Gresham, Acushnet, Seneca,* and *Mohawk* (the U.S. Revenue Cutter Service would become, six years later, the U.S. Coast Guard). The *Acushnet* was busy at the time assisting

Nantucket, a steamer that had run aground off Newport, but the rest of the ships communicated their intent to steam for the wounded *Republic*.

Never before used to signal a ship in distress the size of *Republic*, wireless communication had proven itself in no uncertain terms. It would also provide the public with a live, "breaking news" event, the first of its kind. The new electronic medium would carry moment-by-moment updates from ship to ship, ship to shore, and from and to anyone with a wireless – newspaper or hobbyist – who was following along. The age of mass media was born.

Captain Sealby, meanwhile, on deck, having begun the evacuation of his ship, must have been debating in his head the odds of staying afloat. The ship was listing slightly but seemed in no immediate danger. Perhaps she could yet be saved. He wired as much to the White Star offices in New York.

Florida was by then in view and, it being decided that she would take on *Republic*'s passengers, lifeboats were filled and the transfer proceeded. There was no telling when the other ships would make it to *Republic*, or even be able to find her in the fog, but Sealby's calm demeanor provided both passengers and crew with a confidence that things were, as much as could be expected, under control. At one point, he addressed a group of passengers on deck, saying, "I do not think the ship will sink. She may go down to a certain point, but it is likely her watertight compartments will keep her from sinking." The news elicited three cheers.

For four hours, from approximately 7:30 a.m. until 11:30 a.m., *Republic*'s small lifeboats were rowed back and forth between the two ships. Eugene Lynch, critically injured, was lowered to one of the lifeboats on a stretcher. The body of his wife along with the body of W.J. Mooney were left behind. (White Star would later make the unlikely claim that the bodies were put into hermetically-sealed caskets.)

It was cold, and it was still foggy. The arduous transfer process was uncomfortable if not downright perilous for the passengers, and back-breaking for the crew. With no electrical power to the winches, the lifeboats, filled with the first group of passengers, were lowered manually. But when the lifeboats returned for subsequent groups, they came alongside the ship and the passengers had to make their way down to them, clambering down *Republic*'s long accommodation ladder, essentially three flights of stairs, as it swayed with the rolling sea while the lifeboats knocked against the hull of the ship. The greatest difficulty, Jack Binns would later report, was "inducing the women passengers to leap at the right moment."[12] Author Alice Morse Earl fell into the ocean and had to be rescued, reportedly by being dragged aboard by her hair. (Her health never recovered from the incident and she would

---

[12] *New York Times*, January 27th, 1909.

die two years later at the age of 59.) It didn't get any easier for the passengers when they reached *Florida* where they had to avail themselves of rope ladders.

Of note, of course, is that the lifeboats could have made the transfer in one trip, rather than having to be sent back and forth, but for one catch: there weren't enough of them to accommodate all of the passengers. But then, with the successful demonstration of wireless summoning a fleet of rescue ships upon demand, and a practically unsinkable ship (or at least one designed to stay afloat for hours, if not days), what need, so went the thinking, for a full complement of lifeboats? One of the sad ironies of the *Republic* incident is that it may have provided affirmation to a tragic train of thought that would cost 1,500 lives just three years later.

When the transfer to *Florida* was finished, Sealby was left with a handful of crew members, including Binns still at work in the wireless room. On *Florida*, the *Republic*'s passengers tried to make themselves as comfortable as possible on a damaged, over-crowded ship. Class distinction took a rare backseat and million-aire Samuel Cupples, owner of a 42-room mansion in St. Louis, ended up sharing lunch with an immigrant family from *Florida*'s steerage. Everyone milled about, looking back at the listing *Republic* and wondering what was going to happen next.

Closing in, but moving carefully due to the stubborn fog, were *Baltic*, *La Lorraine*, and *Furnessia*. *Gresham*, out of Provincetown Harbor, was on her way, too. So was *Cushing*.

Mohawk, making for *Republic*, ran ashore in the fog not far out of New Bedford where she was stationed. *Seneca* and *Lucania* steamed for *Republic*, communicating via wireless with both *La Lorraine* and *Baltic* the whole way.

Baltic would steam into the general area first, early in the afternoon, but it would take most of the rest of the day, due to the fog, to locate *Republic*. At 7:20 p.m., from his wireless room, Binns heard a cheer, much too loud to be coming from the eight crew members still aboard *Republic*. Through his cabin he could see *Baltic*. In the dark, the two ships had been firing rockets to ascertain the others' whereabouts and trading wireless messages. What Binns heard were *Baltic*'s passengers, pressed up against the rails, cheering the discovery of *Republic*. Binns wired the land station on Nantucket with which he'd been keeping in contact: *Great guns! Baltic looks good to me!*[13]

La Lorraine showed up very shortly afterwards and then *Lucania, Seneca, Furnessia*, and *Gresham*. It was more than twelve hours after the collision and *Republic* was still afloat. Standard Oil's cargo ship *City of Everett* arrived, along with the company's barge No. 94, and the ship's captain, Thomas Fenlon, communicated to Sealby his willingness to help. His barge capacity was 6,000 tons, more than enough for any baggage or cargo, and he

---

[13] *Modern Electrics* (February, 1909, pages 387-388) reported that their recitation source was Binns's wireless log. However, Binns was quoted in the *N. Y. Herald* (January 26, 1909, 4:1) that he was unable to keep a log. It's more likely that this log was cobbled together from various stations monitoring the transmissions.

had pumps available capable of moving two-million gallons of water an hour. Sealby declined, "curtly", as Fenlon would later recollect.[14] Sealby replied that his ship was doing all right and the revenue cutters would be able to provide sufficient aid.

The good news was that by then the fog was beginning to finally lift. The bad news was that a driving rain had begun. And it was in that cold, driving rain that the process would begin for the transfer of passengers (all of them – *Republic*'s as well as *Florida*'s) to the much bigger *Baltic*. All through the night, already exhausted crew members rowed lifeboats back and forth through a rolling swell between *Florida* and *Baltic*. Eighty-three boat loads in total. Ten hours. Sixteen hundred people.

One passenger initially refused to be transferred. Eugene Lynch, slowly dying of his injuries declared that if he had to die, "I would just as soon go down on *Florida*."[15] He would survive for two more days, dying January 26th in a Brooklyn hospital.

At 9:00 a.m. Sunday morning, Fenlon of the *City of Everett* offered his ship's services once more but again Sealby declined. At 10:45 a.m., loaded with weary, cold passengers, *Baltic* – believing *Republic* could successfully be brought into New York under tow[16] – left *Republic* and steamed for New York. Captain Sealby, still in command of a ship now drawing close to forty feet aft, had

---

[14] *New York Times*, "Could Have Saved Republic, He Says", January 27th, 1909, p.1.

[15] *New York Times*, January 26th, 1909, p. 1.

[16] Ibid, p. 2:1-2.

been in communication with U.S. Revenue Cutter *Gresham* which had been standing by. It had been decided that *Gresham* would attempt to tow *Republic* to New York with help from *Furnessia*. By early afternoon, *Gresham* and *Furnessia* began making fast to *Republic*, *Gresham* to her bow, *Furnessia* to her stern. Steel hawsers were attached, paid out by lengths of rope cleated to the rescue boats, rope that could be quickly severed with an ax should *Republic* go under. Late in the afternoon, *Florida* began limping her way towards New York. At a little after 6:00 Sunday evening, 36 hours after the collision, *Gresham* began towing *Republic*, *Furnessia* following behind.

At the same time, in the second-floor offices of the Bowling Green Building on Broadway in New York City, the officers of the International Mercantile Marine Company were gathered together in a conference room as they had been since the first reports of the collision. A messenger boy had been running in and out with the latest bulletins; wireless reports had been received and sent. The officers of the company were able to communicate with *Baltic*, and also with Sealby. The public had been made aware and newspaper headlines were heavy with the story. Reports had come in about the transfer of passengers and about the rescue attempt of the ship itself. Vice President of White Star, Philip A.S. Franklin, issued a statement saying that, "While the Republic is seriously damaged, we have every hope of saving her."[17] From the safety of dry land, that possibility must have seemed nearly inevitable.

Fifty miles south of Nantucket, the possibility was slowly diminishing. *Gresham* had made little headway over the course of an hour and a half, even with *Seneca* tying up to *Republic*'s bow helping *Gresham* to tow. *Republic* had begun to draw more and more water. With the ship now heavily listing from the stern, *Furnessia*'s line broke, and the choppy seas forced *Gresham* and *Seneca* to reduce speed. *Republic* was going down. Sealby ordered the rest of the crew off, sending them in lifeboats for *Gresham* and *Seneca*, and remained aboard with only the second officer, R. J. Williams.

The two would stay aboard until 8:07 p.m. when there would be no more ship on which to remain aboard, at least above water. From the sinking bridge deck, Sealby fired five shots into the air from his revolver, a prearranged sign for *Gresham* and *Seneca* to disengage their lines from *Republic*. Lifeboats with lanterns were dispatched from both cutters to pluck Sealby and Williams from the icy water. The two had become separated as the ship went down. For Sealby's part, he had managed to climb a hundred feet up the foremast from where he fired one more shot from his revolver.

"Then everything dropped and I was in the water with

---

[17] *New York World*, January 24th, 1909, p. 2:5.

the foremast slipping down beside me like an elevator plunger," he later related in *The* (Fort Covington, NY) *Sun*. "I went under, but came up again, for the air had gathered under my greatcoat and buoyed me up. I guess I went around spinning for a time; then I hit a spar. From the spar I managed to get to a hatch cover. Things were flying around in the water and I came near being badly banged up before I managed to pull my body up on the hatch cover and lie there all spread out with nothing but my head and shoulders above the waves. It was very cold. I saw the searchlights on the *Gresham* and *Seneca* trying to pick me up, but they went around and around and missed me. I managed to load my revolver again and it went off…Soon after that a boat manned by four of the *Republic*'s crew and four sailors from the *Gresham* slid up near me…I was weak and cold – quite finished. Williams was in the boat when it picked me up, I was glad to see. He was quite done up, too."[18] In the same article, *The Sun* also reported this: "One thing (Captain Sealby) did not tell was why he had elected to stay with his ship until it sank."

In any event, 39 hours after the collision, *Republic* was gone.

It remains a matter of speculation as to what was said in that conference room on Broadway when the messenger boy came in with the latest report, a wireless sent by Binns upon Sealby's

---

[18] *The Sun*, "Captain Tells of the Wreck," February 4th, 1909, p. 1.

53

order at 10:31 p.m.: "White Star line, New York: *Republic* sunk. All hands saved. Sealby." Captain J. B. Ranson of *Baltic* had wired in that he thought *Republic* would be saved. The last he'd seen her, she was afloat and ready to be towed into port. Before making for New York, Ranson had called out to Sealby with his megaphone, asking if *Baltic* should remain standing by. "You can go on," Sealby had shouted back, "we're all right." The men in that room must surely have clung to that idea. In fact, plans had already been formulated to tow *Republic* from port to Erie Basin, Brooklyn, to be temporarily patched up and then on to Newport News for final repairs. Now, *Republic* was gone. After the shock, attention must certainly have turned to what, exactly, the loss would mean. Three lives were lost aboard *Republic* and the ship herself was estimated to have a value of $1.5 million, one million of which was self-insured by White Star.

And then of course, there was the cargo.

CHAPTER FIVE

Rumors

"Watched the men who rode you,
Switch from sails to steam.
And in your belly you hold the treasure
That few have ever seen,
Most of them dreams,
Most of them dreams…"

— Jimmy Buffet, "A Pirate Looks at Forty"

"I guess the lot was worth about $25,000," said Samuel Cupples, talking to a reporter about the clothes and jewelry that he and his daughter and granddaughters had lost aboard *Republic*. But then he added, "It was mighty cheap to get off that easily."[19]

Immediately after the collision, everyone had hastily made his or her way topside. At that point, the passengers knew only that the ship had collided violently with something and that the

---

[19] *New York American*, January 26th, 1909, p. 6:3.

power was out and their cabins were dark. The possibility of sinking must certainly have crossed their minds. They grabbed whatever clothing they could put on and went up top, locking their
cabins and leaving everything else behind.

Once on deck, the passengers were kept reasonably calm
by the crew of *Republic*. Captain Sealby had expressed the ship
was in no immediate danger of sinking (if she would sink at
all – she might be able to remain afloat indefinitely), but passengers were made to prepare to board the lifeboats as a precaution.
Nobody was granted permission to return to his or her cabin.
General Brayton Ives sent his valet back to his stateroom to retrieve some of his clothes, but the valet returned empty handed
reporting that he'd been prevented from accessing the room by
ship's order.[20] Not only did Sealby want all the passengers up on
deck so as to begin boarding the lifeboats, but he couldn't risk
allowing people to go wandering back through the stairs and
corridors of the ship in the pitch black. Stewards were dispatched
throughout the ship to make certain everyone was topside and tal-
lied, then they made sure that each cabin was locked behind them.

Milling about on deck, it must have seemed to the passengers that their personal belongings were secure below and
that they would be able to retrieve them later, after the ship was
deemed safe and the power restored. Those thoughts were most

---

[20] *Evening World*, January 25th, 1909, p. 5:6.

likely dispelled once the passengers found themselves being transferred to *Florida*, but once word got out that *Republic* was going to be towed into New York, the passengers naturally assumed they'd be able to pick up their belongings there.

Upon arrival of *Baltic* at New York and hearing the news of *Republic*'s demise, the passengers all seemed to echo Cupples's sentiment. Said James Ross Mellon, "We brought nothing away from the wrecked boat except the clothes on our backs, and even those were a varied assortment of odds and ends, but nevertheless we are happy and thankful."[21]

The general opinion was that the *Republic*'s crewmembers were to be hailed as heroes. Sealby was cheered when he eventually made it to port. Jack Binns became something of a legend with his work in the wireless room, even warranting a ticker-tape parade down Broadway. Interestingly, Binns was offered the opportunity to serve as wireless operator on another White Star ship three years later: *Titanic*. He declined, personal circumstances getting in his way. Greaser Thomas McInerney wasn't quite as lucky; he would take the job offered to him on *Titanic* and the decision would cost him his life.

As to what remained behind of the passenger baggage aboard *Republic*, first-class passenger Mrs. Herbert Griggs reported losing $10,000 in jewels. Mary Smoot lost jewels, too. Alice

---

[21] *New York Sun*, January 27th, 1909, p. 5:2.

Earl lost a sable coat. Reverend Dr. John Morris reported that he had spoken to one man who had lost $4,000 in cash and $25,000 in bonds. All told, claims would be filed for close to half a million dollars in lost personal property. Ninety-six claims exceeded $1,000 each, and of those, 17 were filed by families claiming losses of over $5,000 each. The four women with Cupples, his daughter and three granddaughters, ended up filing a claim for $31,688, a little more than Cupples's original rough estimate to the reporters.

These were no piddling amounts. This was 1909 when the average worker made about $300 per year. The average wage was twenty-two cents an hour. Sugar was four cents a pound and coffee fifteen. Eggs were fourteen cents a dozen. Samuel Cupples's loss would be equal to about $750,000 in today's dollars. The half million dollars in total passenger claims? About $13 million.

Of course the list of lost personal property doesn't include that which had not been declared prior to setting sail. Under the Harter Limitation of Liability Act, enacted by Congress and designed to foster the growth of merchant shipping (and still in effect to this day, at least in part), steamship companies were specifically exempted from any liability for lost items of "... platina, gold, gold dust, silver, bullion, or other precious metals, coins, jewelry, bills of any bank or public body, diamonds, or other precious stones" and any valuable objects "contained in any parcel, or package, or trunk [shipped] as freight or baggage" unless the items were specifically entered on a bill of lading.

Without a specific declaration made by a passenger and confirmed by White Star, the company was liable to each passenger, as it said in black and white on the passenger ticket, for no more than $100. Passengers, however, were free to seek their own insurance against loss of valuables prior to traveling with White Star and probably more than a few did, even with transatlantic crossings having become commonplace aboard steamers like *Republic*, considered safe and highly unlikely to sink.

Henry Savage Landor, a passenger aboard *Baltic*, being quoted in *Harper's Weekly* a couple weeks after the sinking, made an interesting observation contrasting the first-class American passengers with the Italian passengers from steerage: "Americans seemed to grudge mostly the loss of jewelry, of money, valuables, or of lately purchased articles of attire, whereas Italians – no matter how poor – mourned chiefly, and in a sentimental way, over some family souvenir which 'babbo ' or 'mamma ' had given, the association for them being more important than the monetary value of anything they possessed. One young Italian told me he had lost everything except one hundred dollars which he had in his pocket, and which he would gladly give if he could only recover from the wreck an old photograph of his dead father. '*Quella era l'unica,* ' he moaned, pathetically, '*non si puo pia rimpiazzare*' ('that was the only one I possessed and [it] cannot be replaced')."[22]

---

[22] *Harper's Weekly*, February 13th, 1909, p. 96.

The personal belongings of the passengers, however, weren't the only cargo on board *Republic*. The ship was scheduled to dock at Gibraltar to rendezvous with Teddy Roosevelt's "Great White Fleet." For more than a year, 16 battleships (hulls painted stark white) had been circumnavigating the globe, showing off the naval power of the United States. It was a trip that would cover more than 43,000 miles including 20 port calls on 6 continents. The USS *Culgoa*, a refrigerated supply ship, had been accompanying the fleet on the journey, but on January 3rd, *Culgoa* had broken off from the fleet and had steamed for Messina, Italy, to donate her supplies to the earthquake-ravaged city. Back with the fleet in Gibraltar, *Culgoa* was planning on having her supplies restocked by *Republic*. Originally, it was Cunard's liner *Carmania* that had been tasked with delivering the supplies but, for some unknown reason, *Republic*, leaving New York one day later than *Carmania*, became the ship of transport.

The supplies for the Great White Fleet, which included large quantities of fresh and smoked meats, turkeys, potatoes, sugar, onions, eggs, and more, were all lost when *Republic* went down. Just how much was lost became something of a question mark. Prior to the news of the collision, both the *New York Sun* and the *New York Times* reported that *Republic* had 500 tons of provisions aboard. The *New York Herald* reported on "more than 500 tons." After the sinking, the *Times* increased its original figure to 650 tons. But the *Journal of Commerce*, in its January 26th, 1909 issue, quoting data directly from the Navy, reported the loss at just 421 tons.[23] Strangely, the U.S. government would eventually file a claim for only 406 lost tons of provisions, 15 tons less than their own original declaration.

The discrepancies might not be at all important. But it's interesting to wonder at what might have made up the difference between what was reported to have been on board and what was ultimately claimed to have been on board. It wouldn't exactly be unprecedented for a navy to clandestinely ship material (guns? ammunition? *gold*?) aboard a civilian ship, in barrels or crates marked as something else.

The matter becomes more interesting the closer one looks. According to the *Journal of Commerce* – using Navy data – the Navy shipped 526 half barrels of smoked ham aboard *Republic* with a *gross* weight (including the barrels, that is) of 84,160 pounds – 160 pounds per half barrel. The U.S. government claimed a loss of 47,449 tons *net* (90 pounds per half barrel). The difference in weight is presumably the barrels, plus salt (each half barrel of ham was packed with 40 pounds of salt). So with 90 pounds of ham and 40 pounds of salt, you had a half barrel filled with 130 pounds of cargo. This leaves 30 pounds of weight for the barrel itself. And yet, according to the U.S. government's own numbers, *14-pound* barrels and crates were used to ship 140 pounds of potatoes each.

---

[23] *Journal of Commerce*, January 26th, 1909, p. 1:2.

That makes a 30-pound half-barrel seem suspiciously heavy.

Let's suppose instead that the empty half-barrels weighed the same as what was used for the potatoes (and why wouldn't they?). That gives us a total of 144 pounds per half barrel (130 for the cargo, 14 for the half barrel). With 526 half barrels aboard, that's a gross weight of 75,744 pounds, not 84,160. That leaves 8,416 pounds unaccounted for.[24]

What, one might reasonably wonder, constituted this more than eight-thousand pounds? If it wasn't the smoked ham that was declared, or implausibly heavy barrels, then what was it?

The ham anomaly might be nothing. Or it might be everything. It's especially interesting to note that the original weight as listed by the government per half barrel of ham just happened to coincide with the weight of a barrel (called a keg) of gold: 160 pounds. Still, the anomaly might never have been worth even considering but for that which started early and has never gone away: the rumors.

They came immediately. The *New York American*, January 25th: "An unconfirmed report has it a large sum of money was on board the *Republic*."[25] The money, so went the rumors, was to be used for the earthquake sufferers, and may have been, according the *New York American* article, "one of the reasons the captain remained on the ship." The *New York Sun* followed up on the report,

---

[24] *See* Appendix, Exhibit I.
[25] *New York American*, January 25th, 1909, p. 2:7.

inquiring as to whether money had been shipped for Italy aboard *Republic*. A White Star representative, perhaps choosing his words carefully, answered that no "such" money had been turned over to the steamship company.[26] That, of course, left the door open for the possibility of money being shipped for somewhere, or something, else.

Regardless, the rumors began and, throughout the years, were never dispelled (and have never disappeared). References of treasure aboard *Republic* kept popping up. In an August 23rd, 1914 article in the *Washington Post*, regarding new diving technology and the prospects of salvaging previously unreachable wrecks, *Republic* is mentioned: "She is in 245 feet of water and has a rich cargo."[27]

Five years later, a Chicago salvage company, Twentieth Century Deep Sea Salvage Syndicate, inquired of the Coast Guard about the rumored treasure, actually meeting with Commodore Commandant Ellsworth P. Bertholf. Bertholf seems like a person who would have been in an excellent position to have known about the cargo aboard *Republic*. He was a celebrated personality of the period, a Congressional Gold Medal recipient, and the Coast Guard's first Captain-Commandant, the highest ranking officer of the Coast Guard at the time. Who can say what was discussed in the meeting? But in a follow-up letter to Bertholf dated

---

[26] *New York Sun*, January 25th, 1909, p. 2:2.

[27] *Washington Post*, August 23rd, 1914, p. 3:4.

February 8th, 1919, W. Schneider, President of Twentieth Century, references $3,000,000 in American Eagle gold coins. "We would like," wrote Schneider, "to know how much information you or your Department could give us concerning [*Republic*'s] location and other general data."[28] Bertholf's reply, dated February 11th, refers Schneider to Captain K.W. Perry, commander of *Gresham*, the ship that attempted to tow *Republic* into port, "as to the exact location of her sinking." As to the $3,000,000 in gold coins, Bertholf's reply is as interesting for what it leaves out as to what it keeps in, namely, a denial. All Bertholf says regarding the cargo is, "you are referred to files of any of the daily papers published at that time."[29]

And so the rumors persisted and so did published references to them. Harold T. Wilkins, writing for *Popular Mechanics* in March of 1928 lists, among other "rich treasure wrecks", *Republic*, "the $2,000,000 bullion wreck...off Nantucket lighthouse."[30]

Two years after Wilkins's piece, a curious Mr. Louis Miller of Brooklyn, New York, aiming to learn exactly what the Coast Guard knew, sent an inquiry regarding the rumored cargo to the Coast Guard[31] and no less a figure than Captain Benjamin M. Chiswell, World War I recipient of the Navy Cross and man

---

[28] *See* Photos & Exhibits, Exhibit-AH.

[29] *See* Photos & Exhibits, Exhibit-AI.

[30] Harold T. Wilkins, "On the Trail of Treasure," *Popular Mechanics*, v. 49 (March, 1928), p. 434-439.

[31] *See* Photos & Exhibits, Exhibit-AJ.

considered to be the father of Coast Guard aviation, wrote back, saying, "Unofficial information at the time suggested that the *Republic* may have had on board $3,000,000 in American Gold Eagles." Chiswell added, "The facts, however, are not known to this office."[32]

What was this unofficial information to which Chiswell referred? Whatever it was, and from wherever it was originally leaked, it continued to stoke the imagination of treasure hunters throughout the 20th century. From the *Washington Post*, June 24th, 1934: "Three million dollars in gold coins lies in the rotting hulk of the White Star liner *Republic*."[33] From the same paper on December 1st, 1935: "At the present all attempts to salvage the $3,000,000 in [*Republic's*] holds have been unsuccessful."[34] From the 1945 book *Treasure Hunter*, authored by Coast Guard Lieutenant H. E. Rieseberg: "And in the strong room was a large consignment of American Gold Eagles, valued at $3,000,000."[35] From the 1957 book *1001 Lost, Buried or Sunken Treasures*: "The S.S. *Republic*, with three million dollars in gold aboard, sank in a collision off Nantucket..."[36]

---

[32] *See* Photos & Exhibits, Exhibit-AK.

[33] *Washington Post*, "Diving Bell Gropes for Lost Gold," Robert Talley, June 24th, 1934, p. M5.

[34] *Washington Post*, "Lusitania's Treasure of Gold and Gems to be Salvaged," Alexander J. Wedderburn, Jr.,December 1st, 1935, p. B6.

[35] Riesberg, H.E. *Treasure Hunter*, NY, NY: McBride and Co, 1945, p. 228-9.

[36] Coffman, F.L. *1001 Lost, Buried or Sunken Treasures*, NY, NY: Nelsons & Sons, 1957, p. 181-2.

From the *New York Times*, July 9th, 1959: "The White Star liner *Republic*, lost off Nantucket Shoals in 1909, carried $3,000,000 in gold eagles."[37] From the 1964 book, *A Guide to Sunken Ships in American Waters*, co-authored by Coast Guard Commander Adrian L. Lonsdale: "Riches beyond most men's wildest dreams – $3,000,000 in American…gold pieces – reportedly lie in the hulk of the liner *Republic*."[38] From *Yankee Magazine*, December, 1970: "Some $3,000,000 in gold eagles couldn't be removed before [*Republic*] went down."[39] From *Lost Treasure Magazine*, January 1976: "This wreck could be called the wreck of the 'golden eagles,' for…she took to the bottom many kegs of United States ten-dollar gold pieces. For 67 years, $3,000,000 worth of golden eagles have lain in the sunken hulk beneath 240 feet of water."[40] From *Skin Diver Magazine*, September, 1980: "In 1909, $3 million in $10 gold pieces went to the bottom of the sea 12 miles S.W. of Nantucket."[41]

The $3 million in gold coins seems to be the common thread running throughout all of the rumors. (Three million dollars, as long as we're adjusting for inflation with the personal

---

[37] *New York Times*, "Maps Give Skippers Chance at Sunken Gold," Clarence E. Lovejoy, July 10th, 1959, p. 18.

[38] Lonsdale, Cmdr. Adrian L., H.R. Kaplan, *A Guide to Sunken Ships in American Waters*, Arlington, VA: Compass Publications, 1964.

[39] Cameron S. Foote, "Broken Water Ahead," *Yankee Magazine*, December 1970, p. 103.

[40] Teddy Remick, "Wreck of the Golden Eagles," *Lost Treasure Magazine*, January, 1976, p.39.

[41] Ellsworth Boyd, "Top 10 [Undiscovered] Wrecks of the East Coast," *Skin Diver Magazine*, September, 1980, 20:1.

property of the passengers, would be worth close to *$80 million today.*[42]) The continued references to lost treasure aboard *Republic* could have been stopped before they were even started, mere days after the sinking. But no matter how they started, the fact is they were fueled by a seeming conspiracy of silence. Nobody denied anything and nobody admitted anything. No one involved in the matter, from the Navy to White Star to *Republic's* crew to a young up-and-coming British politician and future Prime Minister who may have been in a position to call for a public inquiry but, for some reason, declined to do so – none of these people were saying a thing.

---

[42] And of course this is based strictly on purchasing power and ignores factors such as numismatic value, the relative value of gold, and the concept of provenance. For a full discussion on what the *Republic's* treasure is *really* worth, please see Chapter 13.

CHAPTER SIX

Silence and Concealment

*"The knowledge that a secret exists
is half of the secret."*

— Joshua Meyrowitz

The conspiracy of silence might have begun even before the sinking. Earl Freeman, an amateur wireless operator from just outside Boston, followed along with the wireless messages being sent to and from *Republic*. But they were "fast and furious," according to a *Boston Herald* report from January 25th and Freeman "could not understand the codes used."[43] Maybe Freeman couldn't understand the codes because he simply lacked sufficient knowledge of general wireless transmission to and from ships at sea. Also, different companies at the time often used different versions

---

[43] *Boston Herald,* January 25th, 1909, p. 3:4.

of telegraphic codes. But it might just be possible that Freeman didn't understand the codes because they were being used to purposely obfuscate the information that was being relayed between White Star and *Republic*.

It's a safe bet that popular contemporary journalist and *Republic* passenger James Connolly might have believed this. According to a *New York Sun* article from January 26th, Connolly, while still aboard *Republic*, had been besieged with wireless inquiries from newspapers for his story of the wreck. Well-respected, eminently credible, and with a front row seat to a monumentally historic event, Connolly had seemingly every newspaper lining up for his account. But Connolly was prevented from using the ship's wireless to reply. And according to the *Sun*, "Mr. Connolly intimated that the reason for this was the desire on the part of [White Star] to suppress details of the disaster...a plot to discredit in advance anything he might write later about the accident."[44]

Nothing but silence came from the crew, each member ordered to keep quiet once the rescue ships reached port. A representative from the Marconi Company came aboard *Seneca* to escort the new hero Jack Binns ashore but Captain Sealby refused to allow it, wanting instead to keep his crew intact for the time being. Binns, though technically employed by Marconi, was still beholden to captain's orders, having signed the ship's articles.

---

[44] *New York Sun*, January 26th, 1909, 3:6, 7.

The Marconi Company would have to content itself by sending a message of congratulations to Binns. All of *Republic*'s officers and crew aboard *Seneca* were confined to their cabins. Once ashore, they said little if anything. Sealby, repeatedly pressed for details by the papers, kept deferring to officials of White Star. "When I get the proper permission to talk," said Sealby, "maybe I will tell you something else." He never did.

This may all have been business as usual. It's not unreasonable to assume that White Star would want to keep its employees from making statements that might later come back to harm the company from a liability standpoint. But the liability question brings us back to the Harter Limitation of Liability Act. Beyond what was declared, the most for which White Star was on the hook was $100 per passenger, regardless of fault.

Additionally, there would be no liability for the six deaths because there were no controlling laws at the time governing the loss of life at sea (and wouldn't be until 1920 with the passage of the Death on the High Seas Act). Finally, according to the Harter Act, even if found at fault, White Star could only be held liable for cargo – declared or undeclared – up to the amount of the value of its vessel. Lying more than 200 feet under water and well beyond the era's salvage technology, *Republic*'s value was exactly zero. *Florida*, on the other hand, still held some worth and if the fault for the wreck could be pinned on the Italian liner, then White Star could make claims against the Lloyd Italiano Company to help offset White Star's passengers' damages. But *Florida's* value wasn't very much. Heavily damaged, she sold at auction for just $175,000, the full amount, then, that White Star had to pay out towards all claims.

What it all meant was that White Star had very little to be worried about where liability was concerned. The biggest claim made was by White Star itself to its own insurance company. So why all the silence? Was there something else that White Star was trying to conceal? Maybe $3 million in gold coins? There were those rumors, after all.

One curious fact points to a possible disinformation campaign begun even before the sinking. It was widely reported that White Star's *Oceanic* delivered $3.5 million to Paris, having left New York on January 13th. But suddenly – and very publically – that $3.5 million was reduced to $3 million, the same amount that was already being rumored to be aboard *Republic*. Somebody, somewhere, fed a line to the *New York Post* that was published on page one of its January 23rd edition: "No gold has been shipped to Paris since the OCEANIC sailed with a $3,000,000 consignment, which arrived just in time to do service in yesterday's Russian loan financing." Why was this considered especially newsworthy on this particular date of all dates, the day after the *Republic* collision? It appears to be an answer to an anticipated question, without coming right out and saying what that question was; namely, was there $3 million on board *Republic*? And yet, the same

New York Post reported, just 11 days earlier, that the *Oceanic* cargo was $3.5 million, not $3 million.[45] Was somebody trying to cover the *Republic* rumor – even before *Republic* would sink – with the *Oceanic* cargo?

Any theory of gold aboard *Republic* would have to address two issues: first, why would the shipment not have been declared with White Star? Second, why would it have been necessary to keep such a shipment secret from the general public? We'll leave the latter question open for the time being. As to the former, it would not have been necessary to declare the cargo for the purpose of collecting from White Star in the event of a sinking *if* the cargo had been insured elsewhere. The passengers had this option, as well, of course. Samuel Cupples, for example, could have insured his daughter's and granddaughters' $31,688 worth of jewelry through private means.

Governments, however, as a matter of fiscal policy, don't use private insurers, opting instead to self-insure against loss. The payment of premiums to cover the assets of the United States government would be overwhelming. And so the government hedges its own bets, creating funds to cover potential asset loss; much more economical than making use of private insurers. So the gold *would* have been insured – self-insured, by the government (by some government, anyway), obviating the need to declare it with

---

[45] *New York Post*, January 12th, 1909, p. 2:3.

White Star before it would have been loaded aboard *Republic*.

Aside from any economic benefits, self-insurance provides another advantage over insurance by another party. You don't have to file a claim in the event of loss, a claim that might be made public. An insurance company's stakeholders are likely to want to know the details of a large claim they're paying out. They might even want to publicize it for promotional reasons. There's a file. A record.

History is replete with examples of self-insured losses at sea that remained out of the public eye. During World War I, the RMS *Laurentic* (a White Star liner, interestingly enough) struck a mine and was sunk on January 25th, 1917. *Laurentic* was carrying gold from Britain to Canada to help pay for British war supplies. Self-insured, the loss wouldn't be made public until 1924, and only then after the British government had successfully salvaged almost 100% of the gold.[46] On June 19th, 1940, while in transit from Auckland, New Zealand to Vancouver, British Columbia, Canada, the RMS *Niagara* also struck a mine and was sunk. Aboard her were eight tons of gold bars, payment for war supplies purchased from the United States. Only after a salvage operation that lasted nearly a year would the nature of the cargo be made public.

Here might be the most illustrative example: The S.S. *Central America*, a gold-rush era steamship, was lost in a hurricane

---

[46] The wreck of the *Laurentic* lies in only about 120 feet of water, within salvageable depths for the time. Even at that depth, however, retrieving the gold from the *Laurentic* reportedly took more than 5,000 dives over seven years.

in 1857. Aboard her was a well-documented cargo of gold, well-documented because most of her cargo was non-government gold and privately insured. The loss was openly publicized in contemporaneous newspaper accounts. At least the privately-owned gold. The rest was (self-insured) government gold and was only rumored to exist. It remained mere conjecture for over 130 years when, finally, after salvage of the *Central America* had commenced in the late 1980s, researchers obtained a document from government files confirming the gold's existence.[47]

A significant advantage, in other words, of self-insuring is the same one the government would have enjoyed by not declaring the cargo in the first place, self-insured or not: discretion. And that brings us to the second issue. Why conceal the (rumored) gold? An obvious reason might be fear of theft or hijacking. That reason evaporates after the fact, after her sinking, unless, of course, *Republic* was in a position to have been salvaged or plundered. But she was not salvageable, certainly not with the technology at the time. The idea would have been nearly unimaginable. So, *if* the gold existed, was there a reason for keeping it a secret beyond merely trying to keep it safe? Perhaps a good way

---

[47] Robert Evans, chief scientist of the SS *Central America* project, comments: "During the 1990 trial, Columbus-America Discovery Group's attorneys obtained a certified copy of a letter written to a researcher around 1970. The veracity of this letter was previously in question, mostly because the original letter was not in possession of many who had copies, and there were many copies of copies. So whether or not it was real or a Xerox forgery was a serious question. The letter addressed the existence of a huge government or military shipment, 600 boxes of fifty pounds each. The certified copy of the letter seems to confirm the shipment's existence, although it remains the sole piece of solid evidence for it."

to start tackling that question would be to ask: for what purpose
was the supposed gold? Where would it have been headed? For
whom? For what reason? In short, cui bono: to whose benefit?

An answer to that may well have come by way of an inquiry. Though White Star (as well as Lloyd Italiano) was limited
in its financial liability, certainly the government would have had
an interest in holding an inquiry into the wreck of two passenger
vessels that resulted in six deaths and sent one ship to the bottom
of the ocean. Inquiries for maritime accidents were mandated
by British law, and were even held for insignificant bumps and
scrapes. *Republic* was the largest and most technologically ad-
vanced vessel lost at sea in history to her time. Serious questions
needed answering, questions about the ship's speed under ad-
verse conditions, bulkhead construction, the efficacy of the wireless telegraphy, and – its absence positively tragic three years later
with *Titanic* – a formal line of questioning about the adequacy
of the ship's lifeboats. The lack of such an inquiry by the United
States or Britain is nothing less than mind boggling. And it provided just that much more curious silence.

Strangely, the French, with no obvious connection to the
wreck, undertook more of an investigation than the United States
or Britain. The French government's ostensible reason for holding
its investigation was to study, as the *New York Times* reported on
February 2nd, 1909, "the entire question of wireless communication with the idea of introducing a bill to oblige French navigation

75

companies to install wireless apparatus on all their ships above a certain tonnage."

If France had no obvious connection to the wreck, Great Britain certainly did. *Republic*, after all, was a Royal Mail Ship. Captain Sealby held his master's license under British jurisdiction. As a matter of policy, his license was immediately suspended pending the requisite inquiry, an inquiry that came under the province of the British Board of Trade. The process was straightforward, according to the Merchant Shipping Act of 1894. Any person who may be able to give an account of the wreck would be summoned for questioning. In addition to queries regarding the incident itself, details of the ships, owners, passengers, *and cargo* would be fair game. Then, according to the Act, one copy of the inquiry's findings would be sent "to the Board of Trade, and another to the secretary of Lloyd's in London, and the secretary shall place it in some conspicuous situation for inspection."

Sealby and 294 crewmembers of *Republic*, along with four passengers, sailed for Liverpool aboard *Baltic* on January 30, 1909, arriving for the inquiry on February 8th. Sealby stayed for a month. What happened in that month remains a mystery. Sealby's time there certainly seemed occupied by something. A letter from a friend, a Miss Bernardy, appears to admonish him, good-naturedly, for disregarding his friends back home:

Dear Captain "absolute",

How are you and what is the Board of Trade doing to you just now, and when are you coming to Rome for a few peaceful and cheerful weeks?

You see, we can stand lack of information about our friends when all is well with them, but we mind being cut out at other times. For we are

Faithfully yours
The "Rubber ball"[48]

Seventy-three years later, in October of 1982, a curious man investigating the rumors of treasure aboard *Republic* would begin seeking records of the British inquiry, writing to Lloyd's, the Board of Trade (now the Department of Transport), and others with any interest or possible knowledge of the inquiry into the sinking of *Republic*.

I came up empty.

Lloyd's had no information. The assistant librarian at the Department of Transport wrote back that "we have no trace of a report of an official inquiry into the loss of the S.S. *Republic*…it seems none was carried out in connection with this vessel." The Titanic Historical Society, writing directly to the Department of Transport on this author's behalf, received this reply: "With regard to the White Star Liner REPUBLIC (we) can find no trace of a

---

[48] Inman Sealby Collection, Vineland Historical Society, Vineland, New Jersey.

Board of Trade enquiry of the incident."

My correspondence with the Titanic Historical Society also produced this from Charles Haas, then the president of the Society:

> "I also checked at the National Maritime Museum, the Public Record Office [now referred to as Britain's National Archives], the Southampton Maritime Museum and the Merseyside Maritime Museum without any great success, as you did. One thing I wanted to find, but could not, was a transcript of the court of inquiry into the loss of the REPUBLIC. (We have same for the TITANIC; it's 959 pages of incredible detail!) ...The [Public Record Office] had the reports of the courts of inquiry for the ATLANTIC, TITANIC and NARONIC disasters, but REPUBLIC was conspicuous by its absence..."

An official explanation for the lack of a formal public inquiry was offered all the way back in June of 1909. The Parliamentary Secretary to the Board of Trade stated that "No formal investigation was ordered into the case, as there was no power to compel the attendance of witnesses from the Italian vessel; and, in their absence, any public inquiry would have been of an ex parte character, and possibly prejudicial..."[49] The question was important enough to be raised again three years later after

---

[49] House of Commons, Parliamentary Debates, 30 June 1909, Vol 7, 379-80.

the sinking of *Titanic*. Realizing that an opportunity was lost by not having an official inquiry into *Republic* three years prior, the Board of Trade was asked again why no inquiry had taken place and offered the same explanation in the House of Commons, *using almost the exact same wording*: "…there was no power to compel the witnesses from the Italian vessel…any public inquiry would have been of an ex parte character, and possibly prejudicial…"[50]

This reasoning – flying in the face of precedent (many inquiries were conducted pursuant to British law under similar circumstances, and even when entire ships and their crews had disappeared and there were *no* witnesses available to testify) – meant effectively that no investigation would take place regarding the largest ship ever lost to the sea up until that time. A Royal Mail Ship, no less. It flies in the face of precedent and it flies in the face of common sense.

Then again, a closer look at the Secretary's words reveals something interesting: no "formal" investigation was "ordered." Curiously, that leaves open the possibility of an informal or unofficial investigation, taking place…where? And for what purpose? Sealby and 294 crewmembers certainly didn't take a transatlantic crossing for nothing. Sealby was there for a month and not, presumably, for his health.

---

[50] House of Commons, Parliamentary Debates, 12 July 1912, Vol. 40, 747.

The truth is, governments hold secret inquiries all the time. Barrie Penrose provides an especially appropriate example in *Stalin's Gold – The Story of HMS Edinburgh and Its Treasure.*[51] Evidence was found years after the fact revealing that Russian admiral Arseni Golovko held a secret inquiry into the 1942 scuttling of the HMS *Edinburgh*. The *Edinburgh* was torpedoed by a German U-boat as she steamed from Murmansk with 4.5 tons of gold bullion from Joseph Stalin as payment to the British for war materials. As with *Republic*, no "official" inquiry ever took place. But it's not reasonable to assume a ship can go down with that amount of government money without some inquiry taking place somewhere.

Just what did the crew of *Republic* know? Had there been a gold shipment on board, why even inform the crew? Generally, only the captain, first officer, and/or purser would have any knowledge of a security cargo. But there's an old saying that you can't keep a secret on a ship. It might well be that it was with the crew where the rumors began in the first place.

Then again, how much did White Star itself need to know about the shipment? If gold was being loaded aboard in barrels marked "ham", for instance, was there any reason, as long as you're not declaring it anyway, to inform White Star or its employees? Interestingly, a series of correspondence in 1914 between

[51] Penrose, Barrie. *Stalin's Gold - The Story of HMS Edinburgh and Its Treasure*, Boston, MA: Little Brown and Co., 1982.

White Star and the Navy Department raises the question of just how much White Star knew about the cargo it was carrying on behalf of the government. White Star sent a request to the Navy to ascertain exactly what was lost. Acting Secretary of the Navy, a young Franklin Delano Roosevelt, rather than answer the question, wrote back asking about the purpose for the query. "It is requested that the Department be fully advised as to the reasons that you desire the information," Roosevelt wrote.[52] White Star replied four days later that it was "purely a matter of accountants' closing this unfortunate affair…allowing us to charge to each account a proper percentage of our attorneys' expenses at New York." Apparently satisfied, the Navy wrote back, though this time it wasn't FDR, saying, "The files of the Department show that in the settlement of this matter the naval stores lost on the *Republic* were valued at $61,191.83 and that the Government received on account of its loss in this instance the sum of $25,658.23."[53]

It seems remarkably odd that White Star even had to ask at all. And the wording in the Department's reply is just as odd. "The files of the department show that in the settlement of the matter…" This is an answer, certainly, but not a very complete one, referencing only what the "settlement" showed in "the files." The letters seem superfluous and if one were so inclined, one might wonder if the letters were produced to, effectively, give evidence

---

[52] *See* Photos & Exhibits, Exhibit-AL.

[53] *See* Photos & Exhibits, Exhibit-AM.

from both sides, five years after the fact, that nothing like, say, $3 million in gold, was aboard the ship. The letters conveniently answer, that is to say, the great unsettled question without having to refer to it.

Which brings us back to the crew. If White Star officials knew of the cargo, then most likely they would have confided it to Captain Sealby. A captain needs to know what's on board his ship and the more valuable the cargo, the more important that knowledge becomes. He needs to keep it safe and out of the reach of other crewmembers and, especially, passengers. He might dedicate a whole portion of the ship to such a cargo. The second-class cabins, perhaps. It will be recalled that second class was left purposely empty. And in the event of a mishap, a collision in fog with another ship, for instance, he'd certainly want to keep order and prevent passengers from wandering around below. He'd issue a directive that everyone remain on deck, even if he felt confident that the ship could stay afloat indefinitely.

If rumors of gold ran unchecked throughout the crew, that might explain Sealby and the crew being summoned before an inquiry. But why England? And, again, why the secrecy? Why would the British Board of Trade want to keep an inquiry quiet and why is there no record of it? What, in other words, was it about this particular shipment of gold – if there was one – that it could not be allowed to be made public?

One man with the answers surely would have been the Secretary's immediate superior, the President of the Board of Trade. And so the real question is: what precisely did Winston Churchill know?

CHAPTER SEVEN

"Not an Accident Worthy of Mention"

"The sense of the razor is to cut away useless or gratuitous ideas in ex-
planation, and to accept the simplest hypothesis
which can explain the data."

— W.L. Reese,
Dictionary of Philosophy and Religion
(Humanities Books, 1996)

Over the years, the rumors of gold, coupled with the deafening silence, if not concealment, from those who would have been in a position to have denied the gold's existence (but never outright did so), has led researchers and treasure hunters to speculate on the possible reasons for the rumored gold's presence. Two historical events that were connected to *Republic*'s destinations have become obvious points of interest. The ship was on her way to the Mediterranean, first to Gibraltar to rendezvous with the Great White Fleet, and then on to Naples, the staging area for the ongoing relief effort for the devastating December '08 earthquake. Could either of these destinations, or both, offer some form of confirmation that a shipment of $3 million in gold coins was aboard *Republic*?

There was, after all, that report from *The New York American* printed the day after the sinking: "an unconfirmed report has it a large sum of money was on board the *Republic* for the Italian earthquake sufferers."[54] Relief funds were being raised all over the world. The Red Cross, presided over at the time by William Howard Taft, Teddy Roosevelt's immediate successor to the White House, appealed to Americans with a statement printed in the January 1st, 1909 *New York Tribune*. "It will serve several admirable purposes," wrote Catherine S. Leverich, secretary of the New York County sub-division of the Red Cross, "if all Americans desiring to help the earthquake sufferers in Italy will send their contributions, no matter how raised – whether individually or through societies – at last through the American Red Cross, which is the auxiliary emergency relief organization of the American people."[55]

Two days later, the *New York Times* wrote an appeal with some eye-catching numbers: "The best medium for the distribution of the [relief] fund is unquestionably the American Red Cross Society. That organization has facilities for the work...and its reputation for promptness and discrimination is well deserved. It

---

[54] *New York American*, January 25th, 1909, p. 2:7.
[55] *New York Tribune*, January 1st, 1909, p. 3:1.

is not unlikely that $2,000,000 or $3,000,000 may be needed in Italy from Americans."[56] And of course, just three weeks later, *Republic* steamed from New York towards Naples.

The loose circumstantial evidence for gold on board the ship for Italian relief efforts, though intriguing, doesn't hold up to closer scrutiny, however. First and foremost, the Red Cross would most likely wire the funds after collecting them, not turn them into gold and ship them across the ocean. Ms. Leverich says as much in the *Tribune* statement. The money is collected and transmitted to the Washington headquarters of the Red Cross "…whence it is cabled by the State Department to the Italian Red Cross, already at work in the ruined field."

An inquiry to the Red Cross itself, by this author, 75 years after the sinking of *Republic*, produced this reply: "Our financial records indicate that the total amount raised by the American Red Cross in the United States was slightly less than a million dollars and that the Italian Relief Fund administered by the Red Cross in Italy received and expended in the neighborhood of $1,200,000."[57]

This is not to say that there might not have been money bound for Italy on board *Republic*. It's probable some of the passengers might well have been carrying personal funds they planned to donate once the ship reached Naples. And of course

---

[56] *New York Times*, January 3rd, 1909, p. 10.

[57] Roy S. Popkin, National Deputy Director Disaster Services, American Red Cross, letter dated January 27th, 1984.

the ship was contributing in its own way by carrying the Navy cargo that was to replace the supplies the Navy had shipped from its own stores, the 400-600 tons of provisions. And it is with the Navy where things get a little more interesting.

Commanded by Rear Admiral Charles S. Sperry, in replacement of the ill Admiral Robert Evans at San Francisco, Teddy Roosevelt's Great White Fleet consisted of 16 battleships, seven smaller "torpedo fleet" destroyers, and five auxiliary ships (two store ships like the *Culgoa*, a repair ship, a tender, and a hospital ship). Total personnel included over 14,000 officers and sailors. The fleet left Hampton Roads, Virginia, on the 16th of December, 1907 and, stopping at various ports of call along the way, steamed south around South America (the Panama Canal wouldn't be finished for seven more years), up the South and Central American coast and on to San Francisco, then across the Pacific to New Zealand, Australia, the Philippines, Japan, Ceylon (now Sri Lanka), through the Suez Canal, across the Mediterranean to Gibraltar (arriving there at the end of January 1909), and then finally across the Atlantic and triumphantly back to Hampton Roads, arriving to much fanfare on February 22nd, 1909, George Washington's birthday. An unprecedented display of military might, the fleet covered 43,000 nautical miles and visited 20 ports on six continents.

The fleet's odyssey wasn't cheap. For operational expenses and payroll, the fleet routinely requisitioned upwards of half a million dollars a month (close to $13 million in today's terms). At various points along the way, Fleet Paymaster Samuel McGowan received funds in gold drawn on Navy accounts maintained at both the New York and San Francisco sub-treasuries. Typically, the funds were dispatched aboard a supply ship, the same ship that might be delivering the fleet's food provisions, for example. Payday for the sailors was always on the 25th and deposits made to McGowan's office usually arrived about midway between paydays, usually the first week of each month. Typically, the funds were requisitioned by McGowan approximately 30 days in advance of the fleet's need for them.

According to a June, 1910 accounting to Congress of the tour, issued by the Navy and prepared by McGowan himself (*Operations of Pay Department of the Atlantic Fleet on Cruise Around the World*[58]), deposits for operational funds and payroll for the last several months of the cruise were made October 4th, 1908 at Manila; November 6th, 1908, also at Manila; December 13th, 1908 at Colombo, Ceylon; and January 9th, 1909 at Port Said, Egypt. Interestingly, no deposit was made in early February even though the fleet wasn't due to arrive back in home port until close to the end of that month.

---

[58] *Operations of Pay Department of the Atlantic Fleet on Cruise Around the World*, Report of Pay Inspector Samuel McGowan, U. S. N. Fleet Paymaster. Presented by Mr. Perkins for Mr. Tillman, June 23, 1910, Congressional Serial 5660, 61st Congress 2nd Session, Senate Document No. 646.

THE ITINERARY OF THE GREAT WHITE FLEET

December 16, 1907 - February 22, 1909

Combined Fleet
First Squadron Only
Second Squadron Only
Ports Visited (1 - 20)

Map adapted from http://commons.wikimedia.org/wiki/File:Great_white_fleet_map.svg

Monies Received By the Great White Fleet

No.	Port	Arrive	Depart	Funds Received	Source
1	Port of Spain, Trinidad	23-Dec 07	29-Dec 07	N/A*	
2	Rio de Janeiro, Brazil	12-Jan 08	21-Jan 08	"	
3	Punta Arenas, Chile	1-Feb 08	7-Feb 08	"	
4	Callao, Peru	20-Feb 08	29-Feb 08	"	
5	Magdalena Bay, Mexico	12-Mar 08	11-Apr 08	"	
6	San Francisco, California	6-May 08	18-May 08	"	
7	Puget Sound, Washington	23-May 08	16-June 08	"	
8	San Francisco, California	22-June 08	7-July 08	$500,000	San Francisco Sub Treasury
9	Honolulu, Hawaii	16-July 08	22-July 08		
10	Auckland, New Zealand	9-Aug 08	15-Aug 08	£80,000	Bill of Exchange, on London
11	Sydney, Australia	20-Aug 08	28-Aug 08	£70,000	Bill of Exchange, on London
12	Melbourne, Australia	29-Aug 08	5-Sept 08		
13	Albany, Australia	11-Sept 08	18-Sept 08		
14	Manila, Philippines	2-Oct 08	9-Oct 08	$350,000	Navy Pay Office, Manila
15	Yokohama, Japan	18-Oct 08	25-Oct 08		
16	Manila, Philippines	31-Oct 08	1-Dec 08	$400,000	Navy Pay Office, Manila
17	Colombo, Ceylon	13-Dec 08	20-Dec 08	£75,000	Bill of Exchange, on London
18	Port Said, Egypt	4/7-Jan 09	5/10-Jan 09	£58,500	Bill of Exchange, on London
19	Gibraltar	31-Jan 09	6-Feb 09	**	**
20	Hampton Roads, Virginia	22-Feb 09		$800,000***	Treasury Dept., Washington, D.C.

* This report focuses on the money requisitions of the second and final legs of the fleet's circumnavigation, under the control of Fleet Paymaster Samuel McGowan.

** In the following report, we present facts that lead us to believe the Republic was carrying both Navy supplies AND a money shipment to meet the fleet at Gibraltar.

*** This was the only money requisition marked "SPECIAL," only to be marked as such when the need was "unforeseen."

In fact, by reconstructing a balance sheet based on the report's own data, a negative balance is revealed by the time the fleet arrived at Hampton Roads.[59] Certainly, some provision would have been made for the early February deposit into the fleet paymaster's office. But why didn't it arrive?

---

[59] *See* Appendix, Exhibit II.

Of equal importance to the fleet would have been that the deposit be not just in gold, but in U.S. gold. Cash disbursements along the way were made in the indigenous currency of whatever port of call the fleet was visiting. For Mediterranean ports, the preferred currency was the British gold sovereign. In fact, according to McGowan's report, the fleet's supply of U.S. gold was to have been exhausted by the time the fleet left Manila, before entering the Mediterranean. But once at Gibraltar, with the single remaining destination being the United States, it would have been necessary that the funds on board, including the upcoming payroll for the sailors, be in U.S. currency. It's reasonable to assume, therefore, that the early February funds (the ones that never arrived) would most likely have been shipped to the fleet from America, more specifically, New York City, the location of the sub-treasury. Conveniently, *Republic* had been scheduled to arrive at Gibraltar on February 2nd, with, of course, the replacement food provisions.

The need for funds, the need for funds in U.S. gold from America, the timing, and the fact that she was headed for the fleet anyway, make *Republic*, at the very least, a logical candidate for courier. The fact that no record exists for the early February disbursement is of particular interest. And then there's this: on January 24th, the exact date of *Republic's* sinking, Admiral Sperry ordered the *Yankton*, the fleet's tender, to precede the fleet back home. The *Yankton* arrived at Hampton Roads on February 17th, was coaled, and then was ordered to Washington D.C., arriving at the Washington Naval Yard on February 19th. There, she received

$800,000 from the U.S. Treasury and steamed back for Hampton

Roads, arriving there on the 22nd to meet the rest of the fleet.

The *Yankton*'s cargo was even trumpeted by the *New York Times*:

"$800,000 in Gold for Fleet," read the headline of February 21st.

"The Yankton Takes Money to Pay the Officers and Men."[60]

Of significance is that there was never any other instance

of the *Yankton* carrying the fleet's funds. That she steamed on

ahead of the fleet to acquire funds from the U.S. Treasury in D.C.

(when, not so incidentally, the routine procedure was for funds to

come from San Francisco or New York) is notably peculiar.

Of further significance was the amount: $800,000. It corre-

sponds to what McGowan would have needed for the month of

February. Why $800,000 instead of the routine $500,000? Because

on December 31st (about the time he would have been expected to

make his February requisition) McGowan was asked, as he stated

in his *Operations* report, "to furnish immediately a working memo-

randum of the quantity of provisions available [from the fleet] for

[earthquake] relief issue." It was determined that the supply ships

Celtic and *Culgoa* could deliver $300,000 worth of food rations,

clothing, and other supplies to Messina, all, naturally, originally

intended for use by the fleet. *Culgoa* left the fleet for Messina on

January 3rd. *Celtic*, a supply ship serving the 3rd Atlantic Squadron,

---

[60] *New York Times*, February 21st, 1909, p. 2:7.

a fleet of fighting units that had remained behind, had originally been scheduled to cross the Atlantic and meet up with the Great White Fleet at Port Said, delivering the provisions and monies necessary until the fleet's arrival back home. With the change of plans, she steamed off on December 31st for Italy.

With *Celtic* and *Culgoa* reassigned to Messina, McGowan's normal monthly requisition of $500,000 had to increase by the amount that was being redirected for earthquake relief. Not coincidentally, the total amount of $800,000 was also the total for Italian relief approved by Teddy Roosevelt himself – $300,000 to recompense the fleet along with an additional $500,000. "I do not think," wrote Roosevelt to Senate Appropriations Committee Chairman Eugene Hale on January 4th – knowing full well by then the amount and purpose of McGowan's February requisition – "it would be safe for me to appropriate less than half a million in addition to the rations on the two supply ships [referring to *Celtic* and *Culgoa*]." On January 5th, H.R. 24832 was approved for the expenditure of $800,000 "for relief of sufferers from earthquake in Italy." In a letter dated January 18th, Roosevelt personally directed Secretary of the Navy Truman Newberry to "expend this money as provided by Congress."[61]

This $800,000 would then cover the $300,000 for supplies previously distributed in earthquake relief, as well as cover

---

[61] *See* Photos & Exhibits, Exhibit-O.

$500,000 in relief that would have been wired, or sent in the form of lumber, blankets, food, etc. The relief workers didn't need gold, after all; they needed supplies they could employ immediately. The fleet, however, needed gold. And Roosevelt's congressional request assured it would be there in time for the February disbursement. After all, it all came out of the same account; Roosevelt designated the Navy Department as the agency to expend the earthquake relief funds. On January 18th, just four days before *Republic* steamed out of New York, the Treasury Department credited the Navy's General Account of Advances for the $800,000. Moreover, a January 15th letter from Roosevelt's Secretary of State Elihu Root stipulated the money was to be paid "in cash."[62]

But then events intervened. And what happened in Gibraltar after the sinking of *Republic* suggests some serious scrambling going on by Paymaster Samuel McGowan, the kind of scrambling a fleet paymaster might have to do to accommodate the loss of half a million dollars' worth of expected monies, not to mention an additional $300,000 in replacement funds. Up until Gibraltar, McGowan's monthly payments were performed meticulously, like clockwork, over the previous 17 months. Now, things had changed.

First, each ship had its own pay officer responsible for paying the sailors on his own ship. These pay officers would requisition funds from the fleet paymaster (McGowan) as needed. And

---

[62] Secretary Root, Department of State letter dated January 15, 1909, National Archives and Records Administration, RG 80, File 27162.

typically, those funds would be paid in gold. On January 31st, for instance, the *Vermont*, asked for $20,000 in U.S. gold.[63] The *Nebraska* asked for $30,000 on February 5th. The *New Hampshire* needed $50,000 on February 18th. Strangely, all these requests were filled, not by gold as was requested, but by checks drawn on the U.S. sub-treasury account in New York. And McGowan even reduced the *New Hampshire*'s request to $40,000. As evidenced by records of the accounting officers on file at the Navy Bureau of Supplies and Accounts (now Naval Supply Systems Command), and confirmed through the records of the Treasury Department's Fourth Auditor (Navy auditor), to which paymasters were required to submit quarterly reports, a $50,000 check would have overdrawn the account. Ultimately, McGowan paid *New Hampshire* an additional $17,000 in gold only after the *Yankton* (the ship sent on ahead) rendezvoused with the fleet at Hampton Roads.

In short, the pay officers of these ships were requesting, and expecting, U.S. gold at Gibraltar to pay their own sailors on time, as usual. Yet all McGowan was able to offer them were checks. At no other point in the entire 18-month world cruise was McGowan forced to issue *checks*.

Additionally, no shore leave was permitted for the sailors at Gibraltar, a popular port of call. To sailors, shore leave was a much-anticipated escape from the rigors of the sea, a chance for

---

[63] *See* Photos & Exhibits, Exhibit-M, for a sample requisition from USS *Vermont*.

them to spend (or squander) some of their hard-earned coin. Denial of shore leave had happened before, at Manila, but with reason, namely, an outbreak of cholera there. There was no reason given for the suspension of shore leave at Gibraltar, although Sperry managed to keep the men busy. "Those not coaling," wrote James Reckner in *Teddy Roosevelt's Great White Fleet*, "participated in a program of athletics, boxing, smokers, and rowing events."[64] The need for cash by the sailors was, at least temporarily, deferred. Payday would not have been until the 25th in any event, but the timing of the suspension suggests a paymaster looking to conserve funds. Sailors, while at sea, often kept their money on account with their respective ship's pay officer, withdrawing it only when needed, such as when they go ashore. Drawing their funds all at once for shore leave at Gibraltar should not have been a problem. What would make it one would have been if the next fleet deposit, due in early February, had not arrived. Then, McGowan's liquidity would have been severely compromised. It would have been especially problematic if some or most of the sailors would have decided to take their withdrawals in U.S. gold, rather than the British sovereigns that were aboard from the time the fleet had entered the Mediterranean. That was a likely possibility given that the next stop was the United States. The exchange rate in Gibraltar, though slightly unfavorable, was good enough

---

[64] Reckner, James, *Teddy Roosevelt's Great White Fleet*, Naval Institute Press, 1988, p. 152.

for the relatively cheap prices there.

On the other hand, shore leave would have also provided the fleet a good opportunity to purge itself of whatever British currency was left aboard, which, according to
McGowan's records, was equivalent to over $26,000. Purging
foreign monies when no longer needed was common practice. There was no reason to keep these funds aboard rather
than pay the sailors with them to spend at Gibraltar, unless, of
course, the goal was simple conservation of the fleet's cash in
whatever currency they had. But keep the British funds aboard
they did, all the way to Hampton Roads.

No matter how the sailors would have requested their
pay, it most certainly would not have been in the form of U.S.
checks. Where in Gibraltar would they cash them? This is why
the ships would request gold when abroad. But checks were all
that would have been available for the sailors given that checks
are what the pay officers received from McGowan for early
February. The bottom line is that if the February shipment of
funds – in U.S. gold – did not arrive as expected, that would
have created for Sperry an almost certain imperative to cancel
shore leave. And shore leave was, in fact, canceled.

Once back at Hampton Roads, the fleet was met by
the *Yankton* with its cargo of $800,000 on February 23rd, just

in time for the payday of the 25th. This timing, in and of itself, is odd. By any and all accounts, and as his own detailed records show in his *Operations of Pay Department* report, Fleet Paymaster Samuel McGowan was nothing if not meticulous and efficient. Exceedingly good at his job, he would ultimately go on to head the Navy Bureau of Supplies and Accounts and achieve the rank of Rear Admiral. (The destroyer USS *McGowan* would be named in his honor in 1943.) It simply would have been out of character for McGowan to have arranged for receipt of the monthly funds a mere two days before payday. What if the fleet had been delayed somewhere for a few days? McGowan himself entered into his *Operations* report a cable he had sent, calling for advance planning from the outset "in order that there may not be any delay or confusion at the last moment...in order that the entire money situation may be satisfactorily provided for...while there is plenty of time."[65] This advance planning, incidentally, was in clear evidence by the continual arrangement for funds to arrive at each provision port. For the entire duration of the cruise, funds failed to arrive at only one such port: Gibraltar.

Moreover, McGowan explains elsewhere in the *Operations* report that the process of payment – from the fleet paymaster to the ships' pay officers and ultimately to the sailors – can take days.[66] This accounts, perhaps, for why, once at Hampton Roads,

---

[65] *Operations*, p. 102-103.

[66] *Operations*, p. 127.

the dispersal of the ships to their respective home ports was de-layed. Nobody went anywhere. The official reason given was that the fleet was asked to supply a landing force for President William H. Taft's inaugural parade on March 4th, 1909. This idea, seeming-ly put together at the last minute, seems also out of character for such a meticulously planned operation as the Great White Fleet's around-the-world cruise. It's more likely that the ships were held up to accommodate the hastily-arranged delivery of funds. And the hasty arrangement can mean one of only two things: unchar-acteristically poor planning on the part of McGowan, or a lost shipment that was destined to arrive early February at Gibraltar, but instead never made it.

Tellingly, McGowan did not sign for the $800,000 at Hampton Roads, even though he signed for every other one of his requisitions when they were ultimately delivered. Instead, the funds were received *and distributed* by the *Yankton*'s paymaster, Brantz Mayer who, according to government archives, had never in his career received more than $10,000 in any given month and, in fact, was only bonded to handle funds up to $15,000.[67] What ex-plains Fleet Paymaster McGowan's non-involvement? Could it be that he refused to sign for a requisition he himself did not place? He would have, of course, had no compunction about signing for the requisition he placed at the end of December, the one that

---

[67] National Archives and Records Administration (NARA), RG143 File 105863.

would have covered February's disbursement. Had the disbursement arrived, that is. But a curious thing about that requisition: *it's missing*. The paymaster reports were audited by the Department of the Treasury and are currently available for public view.[68] But in a very tall stack of requisitions within the records of the Bureau of Supplies and Accounts, one in particular that was associated with the Great White Fleet's around-the-world cruise is missing: the one that most certainly would have been made at the end of December, 1908.

What's present instead is the requisition for $800,000 made on February 16th in advance of the February 22nd arrival of the fleet at Hampton Roads. And that requisition, made by the U.S. Navy Paymaster General, is marked "Special," a term reserved, according to the "Memoranda for the Information and Guidance of Commandants and Heads of Departments of Navy Yards and Stations, Commanding Officers of Ships, Engineering, Navigating, Pay Officers, Etc."[69], for when "it (is) not possible to foresee the needs."[70] It strains reason to imagine Paymaster Samuel McGowan unable to foresee a need for monthly funds the likes of which he had been requisitioning every 30 days for the preceding 15 months.

---

[68] *Money Requisitions*, Records of the Bureau of Supplies and Accounts, RG 143, General Correspondence, File Number 99000.

[69] "Memoranda for the Information and Guidance of Commandants and Heads of Departments of Navy Yards and Stations, Commanding Officers of Ships, Engineering, Navigating, Pay Officers, Etc.", Congressional Information Series, N2007-1.94, No. 94, January 2nd, 1909.

[70] *See* Photos & Exhibits, Exhibit-AG.

Timing of Fleet Payments

Oct. 4, 1908: At Manila, fleet receives funds for October.

Nov. 6, 1908: At Manila, fleet receives funds for November.

Dec. 13, 1908: At Colombo, Ceylon, fleet receives funds for December.

Dec. 31, 1908: McGowan requisitions $800,000.

Dec. 31, 1908: *Celtic* leaves New York for Messina.

Jan. 4, 1909: Roosevelt asks Congress for $800,000.

Jan. 5, 1909: $800,000 approved by Congress.

Jan. 9, 1909: At Port Said, fleet receives funds for January.

Jan. 15, 1909: $800,000 is directed to be paid "in cash" to the Navy.

Jan. 18, 1909: Roosevelt directs Newberry to "expend money."

Jan. 22, 1909: *Republic* leaves New York.

Jan. 24, 1909: *Republic* sinks.

Jan. 24, 1909: *Yankton* is sent to U.S. ahead of fleet.

Jan. 25, 1909: Scheduled payday for sailors.

Jan. 31, 1909: Fleet reaches Gibraltar. No evidence of funds received. Shore leave is canceled.

Jan. 31, 1909: *Vermont* is paid by check.

Feb. 2, 1909: Date *Republic* was scheduled to meet fleet in Gibraltar.

Feb. 3, 1909: *Culgoa* leaves fleet for Messina.

Feb. 5, 1909: *Nebraska* is paid by check.

Feb. 16, 1909: "SPECIAL" requisition is made by U.S. Navy Paymaster General for $800,000.

Feb. 18, 1909: *New Hampshire* is paid by check.

Feb. 19, 1909: *Yankton* receives $800,000 at Washington D.C.

Feb. 22, 1909: *Yankton* meets fleet at Hampton Roads.

Feb. 23, 1909: Ships receive funds, just two days prior to payday.

Feb. 25, 1909: Payday for sailors.

Mar. 4th, 1909: Taft's inauguration, for which ships and sailors are bound over.

For February's funds, McGowan accounts for his requisition in the *Operations of Pay Department* report by writing, "Estimating that $1,000,000 would be needed by the fleet on its arrival at Hampton Roads, I submitted requisition therefor and requested cable advice as to the action taken."[71] Later in the *Operations* report, he identifies his request as being $800,000, the amount the *Yankton* delivered. What's interesting is what's conspicuous by its absence. Everywhere else in the *Operations* report, McGowan went to great lengths to detail the fleet's needs and the various transactions. McGowan knew, and recorded, how many pounds of butter were on each ship. He knew how many potatoes there were, down to the potato. And of course his *Operations* report was presented in June of 1910, almost a year and a half after the fleet steamed into Hampton Roads. It wasn't as if additional details were unknown by then to McGowan. Yet no breakdown is entered into his report.

Just as interesting was the copy of the cablegram McGowan entered into the report confirming his request. Secretary of the Navy Newberry had wired back: "Funds required McGowan's requisition December 31st will be supplied."[72] Besides confirming the requisition's date (a *missing* requisition, bear in mind), Newberry's cablegram, coupled with McGowan's entry into the *Operations* report of his "estimate," is surprising by the

[71] *Operations*, p. 108.
[72] *Ibid.*

fact that its entry is made with no further explanation or details. Two sentences – McGowan's note about making the requisition and Newberry's cabled confirmation, which is undated – were all that were entered into the *Operations* report about the single largest requisition of money made at any time during the fleet's entire around the world cruise. Bear in mind that, with McGowan, we have a man who documented with page after page receipts and disbursements down to the potato. Yet the largest payment the fleet received was mentioned in just *two sentences*, and which were included in a report submitted more than a year after the fact. Questions the missing details leave unanswered would, of course, include where the funds were to be distributed, to whom, in what form, and when. McGowan's report is chocked full of those details for every other transaction.

Congress of course, being presented with McGowan's *Operations* report, could have asked these questions of McGowan, except for one minor detail: the report was submitted on McGowan's behalf. McGowan was out of the country at the time.

Trying to explain away the odd timing of the receipt of the funds, McGowan attempts to convey in his *Operations* report that the $800,000 delivered by the *Yankton* at Hampton Roads was for both February *and* March's disbursement requirements. And yet, this idea is refuted by records of the accounting officers on file with the Treasury Department.[73] Requisitions were made for the month of March to either McGowan or Paymaster General E. B. Rogers by the *Louisiana* ($35,000 on March 5th), the *Wisconsin* ($30,000 on March 5th), the *Kearsarge* ($20,000 on March 9th) the *New Hampshire* ($25,000 on March 9th), the *Connecticut* ($35,000 on March 10th), the *Ohio* ($25,000 on March 10th), the *Rhode Island* ($25,000 on March 11th), the *Kansas* ($25,000 on March 13th), the *Illinois* ($25,000 on March 23rd), the *Connecticut* again ($35,000 on March 25th), the *Panther* ($12,000 on March 26th) and the *Louisiana* again ($30,000 on March 27th). McGowan himself received $200,000 for the fleet on March 3rd.

Tellingly, none of this money is discussed in McGowan's *Operations* report.

Let's break this down into a brief summary. There is no record of a timely February disbursement to the fleet, even though the fleet received around half a million dollars at the beginning of every month since it had set sail. Fleet paymaster McGowan would have needed $800,000 in early February to cover the standard half a million, plus replace the $300,000 that had been sent to Messina on the *Culgoa* and *Celtic*. He would have needed it in U.S. gold since the United States was the next stop. *Republic* was due to meet the fleet in Gibraltar on February 2nd with a reported 650 tons of Navy provisions. Teddy Roosevelt made certain that

---

[73] *Money Requisitions*, Records of the Bureau of Supplies and Accounts, RG 143, General Correspondence, File Number 99000.

$800,000 was available to the fleet by January 18th. McGowan paid the fleet's ships in February with checks, not in cash as was standard procedure, or, more particularly, in U.S. gold as was specifically requisitioned by the ships. Shore leave at Gibraltar, a popular port of call and a potential source of fund depletion, was canceled. McGowan's December 31st requisition for February, though referenced, is missing. His explanation for the $800,000 required at Hampton Roads is, in practical terms, also missing. His suggestion that the $800,000 was earmarked for two months (February and March) is refuted by official records elsewhere. The $800,000 at Hampton Roads was received 1) by the *Yankton*, 2) in Washington, and 3) distributed to the fleet a mere three days before payday, *all* of which are odd. And McGowan didn't sign for the receipt of the funds that he supposedly requisitioned.

It becomes fairly impossible to explain away the whole of this without invoking the philosophical principle of "Occam's razor", and using the simplest, most obvious, perhaps only, explanation available: gold funds in the amount of $800,000, expected by the fleet in Gibraltar in early February, never arrived having been lost at sea aboard *Republic*.

But then comes the question of secrecy. Why go to such lengths to keep the fact that $800,000 in gold earmarked for the Navy was lost? The answer might have been simple embarrassment. Teddy Roosevelt was proud of the Great White Fleet's accomplishment, returning from its around-the-world tour "without a scratch," as he put it. "You have falsified every prediction of the prophets of failure," he said in a speech addressing the fleet on the day it sailed into Hampton Roads. "In all your long cruise not an accident *worthy of mention* has happened to a single battleship, nor yet to the cruisers or torpedo boats"[74] (emphasis added). The extravagant tour with its associated costs was not without its critics. Roosevelt would have been loath to admit to almost a million dollars lost on account of it. The Navy department itself must certainly have felt the same way. Earlier, in fact, on January 24th, after the collision but even before *Republic* sank, the *Brooklyn Union Standard* reported this: "Navy Department officials at Washington say that the loss of the supplies [at least the known food provisions aboard *Republic*] will not embarrass the fleet, as they were in the nature of an 'extra shipment' for use in the event of an emergency."[75] A preemptive answer to an anticipated question about the tour being somehow tainted by the loss?

Of course the loss of Navy funds would have fallen well short of the rumored $3 million. $800,000 is no piddling amount, however. If nothing but that is resting aboard *Republic*, it's worth over twenty million in today's dollars to whoever can get it. And that's just using purchasing power to calculate the relative value. In numismatic value, its worth is easily at least $70 million.

---

[74] Also note Roosevelt's comment surrounding the 1902-1903 Venezuela Crisis, "not a cloud on the horizon." *See* Chapter Eight.

[75] *Brooklyn Union Standard*, January 24th, 1909, p. 6:2.

Still, $800,000 in gold in 1909 dollars isn't $3 million. Could the rumored $3 million have been on board for something else? And if so, does that provide another reason for the secrecy? Why was the Navy – why was Teddy Roosevelt – so intent on making sure nobody had reason to look very closely at that which did not show up in Gibraltar early that February of 1909 aboard the RMS *Republic*?

PHOTOS & EXHIBITS

THE SHIP

The RMS *Republic*, a palatial steamer at 15,400 tons and 570-ft in length. She was one of the fastest and most luxurious ships of her day.

Exhibit-B

The First Class entrance, looking across the ship to port.

The First Class Dining Saloon, with seating accommodations for no fewer than 200 passengers.

Exhibit-C

Because of the rich and famous who traveled by her, the *Republic* became known as the Millionaires Ship.

The elegant stained glass dome and wood-carvings resting above the First Class Dining Saloon.

Postcards

Republic leaving Genoa

Republic from Liverpool

The RMS *Republic* carried not only wealthy passengers but also mail and other cargoes to various destinations (per her "Royal Mail Ship" designation). She held the record for the fastest passage between Queenstown and Boston and Boston and Queenstown.

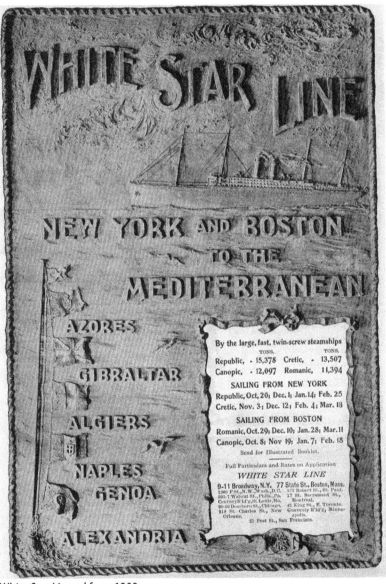

White Star Line ad from 1908

Although many credit this photo as being of the White Star Liner *Republic*, it is actually of the White Star Liner *Canopic*. The decks of the ships were nearly identical with the large, single funnel and a number of lifeboats in the background.

Captain Inman Sealby was the captain of RMS *Republic*. Sealby would lose his license as a result of the sinking and go on to become a maritime attorney, but he would never have a chance to clear his name because the lack of a public Inquiry into the loss of *Republic*.

Captain Sealby of the RMS *Republic* (left) standing with Captain J.B. Ranson of RMS *Baltic*. The *Baltic* assisted with the transfer of passengers from the sinking *Republic*, but was refused any attempt to salvage the injured ship itself.

Exhibit-F

THE GREAT WHITE FLEET

The *Connecticut* leads the fleet out of Hampton Roads.

Teddy Roosevelt's Great White Fleet, composed of 16 battleships and 14,000 sailors, traveled more than 40,000 miles circumnavigating the globe on an unprecedented 18-month world cruise. The ships departed Hampton Roads, Virginia on the 16th of December 1907, and returned on the 22nd of February 1909. The *Republic* departed on her final journey on the 22nd of January 1909, bound for Gibraltar with a documented cargo of supplies for the Fleet.

The *Kansas* sails ahead of the *Vermont* as the fleet leaves Hampton Roads.

President Roosevelt overlooks the departure of the Fleet from the U.S. Presidential yacht *Mayflower* off Hampton Roads in 1907.

The Great White Fleet's journey had its share of both supporters and critics. The supporters heralded the fleet as the "Nation's Pride," an exhibit of American naval dominance. The critics found the journey a major unnecessary expenditure.

Exhibit-H

Above – "Don't be afraid Uncle. – We'll get there all right!" – 1907
Below – "The Nations Pride" - 1908

Exhibit-I

THE GREAT WHITE FLEET
CHAIN OF COMMAND

Theodore "Teddy" Roosevelt
U.S. President

Roosevelt ordered the circumnavigation of the Great White Fleet in order to exhibit the power of the United States Navy. Roosevelt had only two weeks left in office upon the Fleet's return to Hampton Roads. Despite the milestone, he discusses little about the Fleet or the Messina Earthquake relief efforts in his autobiography, nor in his "letters" publicly available at the Library of Congress.

Samuel McGowan
Paymaster of the Fleet, Ship Paymaster of USS Connecticut

McGowan was solely responsible for requisitioning money for the fleet to cover payroll and expenses each month. He was consistently meticulous in his accounting and issuance of comprehensive reports, with the single exception of the largest requisition of the Fleet (marked SPECIAL), the $800,000 requisition of February monies to be delivered to the Fleet at Gibraltar. In accounting for that missing requisition, he only wrote a few sentences many months after the fact.

Truman Newberry
Secretary of the Navy

Charles S. Sperry
Rear Admiral of the Navy, Commander-in-Chief of the Atlantic Great White Fleet

The *Connecticut*. The hulls of the ships were painted white to reflect peacetime and be visible from afar.

Each ship had its own ship paymaster. McGowan was paymaster for the entire Atlantic Fleet and also his own ship, the *Connecticut*. Payroll funds were generally received the first week of the month for that month's disbursement. McGowan was not only responsible for distributing money to the 800-plus men on his own ship, but also to ensure that each ship in the 16-plus ship fleet received its disbursement to pay its men on the 25th of each month.

The Fleet passing through the Straits of Magellan, rounding the tip of South America during the first leg of their world cruise. The money for the Fleet generally followed the provisions when the ships reached designated ports of call.

To request money for his own ship, each paymaster submitted a money requisition to McGowan for the funds that he expected to receive for his ship (to cover payroll and operating expenses). Here is a very peculiar requisition I uncovered from the USS *Vermont* that was asking for $48,000 in U.S. Gold for the pay period February 22nd – March 31, 1909. Remember that payroll monies generally came in the first week of the month, which, coincidentally, was when the *Republic* was scheduled to meet the fleet at Gibraltar with a large cargo of Navy supplies from the U.S.

Exhibit-L

U. S. SHIP ___V E R M O N T___, ___First___ RATE,

Manila Bay, Philippine Is., ___November 18___, 190 8

Sir:

There is required for disbursement in the Pay Department of this ship the sum of ___Forty eight thousand___ - - - - - - - - - - - - - - $\frac{X}{100}$ dollars,

in ___U.S.Gold___, viz:

General account of advances.. $48000.00

Amount of cash in hand ___Manila___ $24000.00
" " " " ___English gold___ 8574.76
~~On deposit with Asst. Treas. at~~ ___American~~ Gs 2011.22

On deposit with Asst. Treas. at ___New York___ $17161.59

Total in hand and on deposit.................... $51747.57

Average monthly disbursement...................... $25415.17

Respectfully,

S B aker

To Pay ~~Inspector~~
___Samuel Mc Cohen___, U.S. Navy   Pay ___master___, U.S. Navy.

U. S. Ship ~~Connecticut~~   Funds required from Feb. 22, '09 to March 31, 1909.

Approved and forwarded: Approved:-- ~~Norfolk National Bank Check.~~

___Captain___, Navy, Commanding Officer.   Rear Admiral, U. S. Navy,
~~Commander-in-Chief~~, S. Navy, Commanding,
U. S. Naval Force ___United States Atlantic Fleet___ Station.

PAID BY CHECK NO. ___2___

ON ___Nof N.B___ DATED _____   Hampton Roads, Va.,
(Place.)

FOR $ ___48.000___   ___February 23___, 190 9
(Date.)
in cash _____

I hereby acknowledge to have received/from ___Samuel Mc Cohen___

Pay ~~Inspector~~ ___W.___, U. S. Navy, upon the above requisition, the sum of

___Forty eight thousand___ - - - - - - - - - - - - - - $\frac{X}{100}$ dollars,

under "General account of advances," for which I hold myself accountable

to the U. S. Navy Department, ~~and have signed triplicate receipts.~~

$48000.00

SB 271 21

Pay ___master___, U. S. Navy.

INSTRUCTIONS.—Pay officers must indorse, both on the face and back of each copy of a money requisition, the word "original," "duplicate," or "triplicate," as the case may be, and the receipt should in no case be signed until

Notice all the items crossed out and re-written. It seems clear that the receipt of the U.S. gold needed for February payroll didn't quite go as planned. See Chapter Thirteen. (*Source: NARA RG 217, Entry 811, Stack 230, (by Paymaster) Baker, C.S.*)

Exhibit-M

The 1908 Italian Earthquake

A photograph depicting the monumental damage at Messina, Sicily.

On December 28, 1908, the most devastating earthquake to strike Europe in recorded history hit southern Italy. The damage was catastrophic, killing more than 100,000 people and leaving hundreds of thousands more homeless. Roosevelt, without first consulting Congress, ordered the Great White Fleet's supply ships to Messina immediately to aid survivors. Relief efforts were quickly underway from all over the world as the news of the disaster spread.

French headline:
"200,000 VICTIMS"

Poster commemorating those lost.

THE WHITE HOUSE
WASHINGTON

January 18, 1909.

To the Secretary of the Navy:

In accordance with the enclosed request from Secretary Root, and further, in accordance with the conversation you and I held with Secretary Root, I have directed the Secretary of the Treasury to turn over to you the $800,000 appropriated by Congress, and I now direct you to expend this money as provided by Congress and as indicated in the accompanying communication.

Theodore Roosevelt

Enclosures

Roosevelt's correspondence to Newberry directing him to expend the (missing) $800,000 on January 18th. The *Republic* was to depart on January 22nd with a cargo of Navy supplies to meet the fleet at Gibraltar. See Chapter Seven. *(Source: Secretary of the Navy to the President, Navy Department letter dated January 18, 1909, NARA, RG 80, File 27162-10, and Note attached to Treasury Warrant No. 16, NARA, RG 80, File 27162.)*

Exhibit-O

AMERICAN TOURISTS ARE ALL

President Offers Fleet and Supplies to Italy

Cargoes of the Culgoa and the Celtic Are Rushed to Messina and the Battleships Will Be Placed at Disposal of Italian Government.

An article showing Roosevelt's decision to send the supply ships of the Fleet to Messina. *Republic* took over *Celtic*'s cargo and delivery to the fleet. The *Celtic* had carried money to ships of the fleet previously. (Source: *New York Herald* – January 3, 1909).

Exhibit-P

PARTMENT,
Division of Bookkeeping and Warrants,
Form No. 523.

APPROPRIATION WARRANT NO. 16 , N A V Y DEPARTMENT.

Treasury Department.

To the Comptroller of the Treasury and the Chief of Division of Bookkeeping and Warrants:

Congress having, by the hereinafter-mentioned Act, made the appropriations thereunder specified, amounting to

————————Eight hundred thousand dollars————————

You are directed to cause this sum to be carried to the debit of the general account of appropriations, and to credit each appropriation with the sum so appropriated, and for so doing this shall be your WARRANT.

Given under my hand and the seal of the Treasury Department, this 18th *day of* January *in the year of our Lord one thousand nine hundred and* nine *and of Independence the one hundred and thirty-* third.

Official Copy:

Chief of Div. of Bookkeeping and Warrants.

Signed _____
Secretary of the Treasury.

Received, recorded, and countersigned January 18th , 1909

(Sgd.) _____
Comptroller.

5—3173

RELIEF of SUFFERERS from EARTHQUAKE in ITALY ⸻ 800,000

Public No. 184. Approved January 5, 1909.

Note:- To be expended by the Secretary of the Navy
from "General Account of Advances," Navy Department, under
authority and direction of the President of January 18, 1909—
adjustments thereunder to be made through the Auditor for the
Navy Department.

See the President's letter of January 18, 1909,

B. & W. 3199 of 1909.

The actual January 18th Warrant for $800,000 to go to the Fleet - $300,000 of which was to reimburse the Fleet for supplies given to earthquake victims and $500,000 for the Fleet's February payroll. We believe that this original $800,000 requisitioned was lost on the *Republic. (Source: Treasury Warrant No. 16, NARA, RG 80, File 27162.)* This is supported by a *second* $800,000 requisition following the loss of *Republic (see* Exhibit-AG).

Exhibit-Q

Postcard with original text: "Sailors From The Battle Fleet Viewing The Ruins of Messina, Sicily, Destroyed by Earthquake Dec. 28, 1908"

THE TSAR'S TREASURE

The last Tsar of Russia,
"Bloody" Nicholas II.

By early 1909, the Tsarist regime was facing substantial difficulty. Russia's loss to Japan in the Russo-Japanese War of 1904-05, coupled with widespread social unrest and talk of revolution, created tremendous financial and political strain for Nicholas II. He was forced to borrow heavily (mostly from France) to repay Russia's war debts and attempt to uphold its crumbling infrastructure.

Exhibit-S

Political Cartoon - "Assez ! – Enough ! – Jeung !" – depicting Roosevelt's mediation role in ending the Russo-Japanese War in 1905. Roosevelt was awarded a Nobel Peace Prize for his efforts (giving him a vested interest in the well-being of both countries).

Postcard depicting the 1905 Russian Revolution.

The original French loan to Russia (that was due in 1909) was refinanced and enlarged to $250 million. The loan was to close on January 22nd, 1909, the exact day that Republic was to sail. Although the loan would close that date, Russia wouldn't receive a single dollar (or franc) of that money for another 30 days, presenting what would likely be an immediate need for cash to cover the 1909 budget.

Actual subscriber bond document for the 1909 4 ½ % Russian loan.

Exhibit-U

TREASURY DEPARTMENT

62344

OFFICE OF THE SECRETARY

WASHINGTON

January 14, 1909

The Honorable

The Secretary of State.

Sir:

I have the honor to inform you that in accordance with the request contained in a letter from your Department, dated the 12th instant, telegraphic instructions were this day addressed to the Collector of Customs at New York, directing him to extend the usual courtesies, including the free entry of his baggage, to Mr. Wilenkin, Commercial Attache to the Russian Embassy to Japan, on his arrival per Steamship "Prinz Friederich Wilhelm" to-day, enroute to his post at Tokyo.

Respectfully,

Acting Secretary.

No enclosures.

The Treasury Department memo providing Gregory Wilenkin, an agent of the Russian Minister of Finance, with diplomatic status upon entering New York. See Chapter Eight. (Source: *National Archives Microfilm Publication M862 (State Dept. correspondence for 1906-1910, arranged numerically by case file number), roll 85, document 17409.*)

Exhibit-V

Mr. Gregory Wilenkin
Russian Minister of Finance Agent

Wilenkin appeared in New York on January 14th, the day before the mysterious $3,000,000, 30-day, low-interest loan was described in New York papers. He departed on January 23rd, the day after the Republic set sail for Gibraltar. He was granted official Diplomatic Status when he arrived in New York.

Wilenkin would have been just the man for the job of procuring a short-term loan in New York.

In addition to the Great White Fleet making its last stop at Gibraltar (and waiting on supplies from the *Republic*), the Russian Baltic Fleet was also in attendance at precisely the same time. A few photographs of the fleets follow.

Russian cruiser ADM. MAKAROV (right) anchored at Gibraltar, as seen from USS *Wisconsin*. January 30th – February 6th, 1909.

Exhibit-W

USS *Kansas* & USS *Abarenda* at Gibraltar with other ships of the Great White Fleet (and Russian ships in background).

Any mention of Gibraltar in U.S. Navy records is nearly impossible to find within the government archives. Given the quantity of records and correspondence at other stops on the cruise, the lack of records for Gibraltar is another instance where the information is conspicuous by its absence, particularly with the correspondence that must have occurred regarding the large loss of Navy supplies while en route to meet the fleet.

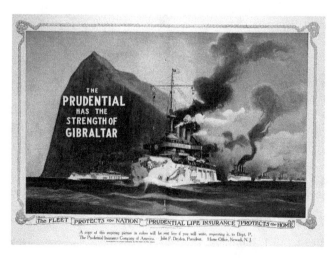

Prudential Life Insurance ad featuring "The Rock" and the Great White Fleet at Gibraltar.

Exhibit-X

Postcard: "GIBRALTAR – View of the Harbour with the British, American and Russian Fleets – 31 January 1909"

Full set of postcards showing all the fleets in a panoramic view of the Gibraltar Harbour – Jan. 31st, 1909.

Exhibit-Y

The "Accident"

The powerless *Republic* sinking stern first with skeleton crew on board. Photo taken from the *Baltic* the morning of January 24, 1909.

In dense fog, at 5:40 a.m. on January 23, 1909, the *Republic* was struck on the port side amidships by the bow of the *Florida*, immediately reducing half a dozen staterooms to rubble and tearing a hole below the water line into her engine room, knocking out her power. Jack Binns, the Marconi wireless operator, immediately began sending wireless distress signals for help as passengers were urged to leave and lock their belongings and arrive on the top deck to await instruction. Binns stayed at his post for 18 hours straight in the cold Marconi room as the ship slowly filled with water.

A young Jack Binns in his Marconi uniform.

The Marconi wireless room aboard the *Republic*.

The *New York* (left) passes by the injured and powerless *Republic*. The *Florida* can be seen in the background (right). Photo taken from the *Baltic*.

A number of ships responded to the "CQD" by Binns. Passengers were first transferred by lifeboats from the *Republic* to the crowded *Florida*, and then later to the *Baltic*. The boiler room and engine rooms were flooded from the collision, knocking out all power to the ship (other than the small back-up power used for the Marconi room). Passengers, leaving their belongings behind, were ushered into lifeboats that had to be manually lowered into the water. The captains of the responding ships presumed the *Republic* would stay afloat.

Republic passengers being transferred to the *Florida*.

The Italian Lloyd S. S. Florida in the Morse Dry Dock, N. Y., after ramming and sinking the S. S. Republic in January, 1909. Jack Binns, wireless operator of the latter vessel became famous when he sent out his C.Q.D. after the collision. The photograph shows the tremendous impact of such a collision.

A photograph of the *Florida's* bow following the collision.

THE AFTERMATH

Everything was a bit chaotic following the *Republic*'s sinking. *Republic* passengers counted their losses, Binns became a national hero, and Roosevelt thought of ways to lessen the impact of the loss of the Navy "stores," as well as perhaps a much larger, politically sensitive cargo.

Top: Headline from *The Evening Telegram – New York*, January 24, 1909.
Left: Samuel Cupples, just one of approximately 250 first class passengers aboard, claimed a loss of $25,000 in gems.

Roosevelt meets with Secretary Newberry and Rear Admiral Sperry upon the Fleet's return.

Roosevelt addresses the sailors of the fleet aboard the *Connecticut* at Hampton Roads. "Not an accident worthy of mention ... "

Meanwhile, back in the U.K., the President of the British Board of Trade, a young Winston Churchill, summons *Republic's* Captain Sealby and his crew for an "unofficial" Inquiry into the accident (despite a formal, public Inquiry being mandated by British law).

Exhibit-AD

With the loss of supplies (and payroll), the Fleet scrambled for cash once back in Hampton Roads. Here's a letter from Admiral Sperry ordering the *Yankton* to go ahead of the fleet the *day* the *Republic* sank (with Navy "supplies") in order to procure money.

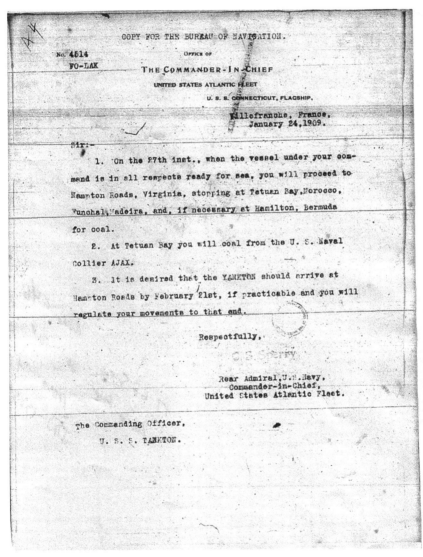

Sperry's letter, sent on January 24th ordering the *Yankton* to precede the fleet back to Hampton Roads. *(Source: NARA RG 45, Area Files of the Naval Record Collection, 1775 – 1910, Area 4, M625 Roll 46.)*

Exhibit-AE

NAVY DEPARTMENT,
BUREAU OF SUPPLIES AND ACCOUNTS,
WASHINGTON, D. C., February 16, 1909.

MEMORANDUM FOR THE DEPARTMENT:

The accompanying requisition is submitted for the purpose of supplying the Atlantic Fleet with sufficient funds immediately upon its arrival at Hampton Roads on February 22nd. The fleet will have no United States money on hand and the funds will be required for immediate disbursement to officers and men.

It is requested that this memorandum be forwarded with the requisition to the Treasury Department, for their information. The U.S.S.YANKTON ~~U S S Detroit~~ will arrive at the Washington Navy Yard on the 19th instant. ~~Assistant~~ Passed Assistant Paymaster ~~Atkinson~~ Mayer will be given full instructions regarding the drawing of these funds from the Treasury on the 20th inst.

~~A list will be prepared showing~~ the denominations of currency which will be required and furnished to the Treasury Department. The necessary instructions have been given to have the necessary boxes made at the Washington Navy Yard in which the money will be packed and sealed for transportation.

E B Rogers
Paymaster General, U. S. N.

Approved:
[signature]
Secretary of the Navy.

The Yankton will take safe from W. to fleet

Notice the names crossed out and changed. Also of note is the location of the money. The Navy had always drawn on its accounts in New York, but for this single transaction they requested money from Washington. Brantz Mayer had never signed off on receipt of any requisition and was only bonded for up to $20,000. Now he was to sign off on $800,000, the single largest disbursement to the Fleet during its cruise. *(Source: NARA RG 217, Entry 811, Stack 230, (by Paymaster) Mayer, Brantz.)*

Exhibit-AF

The Fleet needed U.S. gold. Some ships had specifically requested U.S. gold at Gibraltar and instead were forced to accept checks. The preceding internal Navy memo, as well as the requsition below, exhibit this urgent need for cash. Such an event seems rather odd for an 18-month world cruise that had been meticulously planned years in advance.

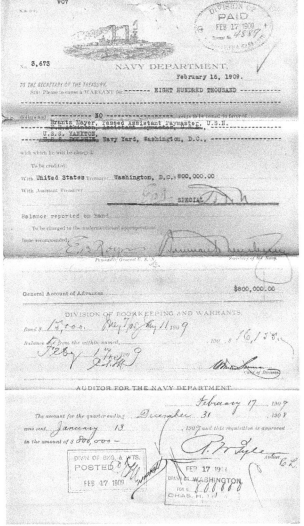

This is the *second* requisition for $800,000 by the Navy, marked "SPECIAL". "Special" was a term-of-art that was to be used only "when the need is unforeseen." *See* Chapter Seven.

(Source: NARA RG 217, Entry 811, Stack 230, (by Paymaster) Mayer, Brantz.)

THE LEGEND

Rumors began to circulate the day the *Republic* sank that "a large sum of money" was on board. These rumors have persisted for more than a century, taunting those bold enough to attempt to collect her fabled treasure.

EMPLOYING SCHNEIDER-LIPSKI SALVAGE EQUIPMENT
(UNDER EXCLUSIVE RIGHTS)

TWENTIETH CENTURY
DEEP SEA SALVAGE SYNDICATE
MARQUETTE BUILDING
CHICAGO

OFFICE OF TREASURER
FRANKLIN PERLOWSKY, TREASURER

February 8, 1919.

Commodore Commandant Ellsworth P. Bertholf,   U.S. COAST GUARD
   Coast Guard,   REC'D
      Bond Building,   ANS'D FEB.11 1919   BY
         Washington, D. C.   FEB 1 1919

My dear Sir:

      Regarding the little session we had with you and Captain McAllister in the course of which reference was made to the White Star Liner containing $3,000,000 in American Eagles,- we should like to know how much information you or your Department could give us concerning her location and other general data.

      The matter mentioned has strongly appealed to the imagination of my associates and myself and if there is any possibility of getting the contract for the salvaging we should like to have a fling at her.

      We have the pleasure of informing you that we were quite successful and believe that within the very near future you will hear and know of some of our activities. We believe that we have aroused your curiosity in our venture to a certain extent and we will in an unofficial way keep you posted as to our progress.

      Again let us thank you for the cordial reception and the courtesies extended to us at the time we called at your headquarters.

              Respectfully yours,

              DEEP SEA SALVAGE SYNDICATE

              By _____
                          President.

WS/H

Twentieth Century Deep Sea Salvage Syndicate describes their 1919 meeting with Coast Guard officers and their discussion of Republic's $3 million cargo. *NARA, RG 26, General Correspondence, File 651 ("RE," includes Republic).*

Exhibit-AH

, February 11, 1919.

The Deep Sea Salvage Syndicate,
    Marquette Building,
      Chicago, Ill.

Subject: Sinking of White Star Liner "Republic".

Reference: (a) Your letter, February 8, 1919 (WS).

Gentlemen:

     1.   Replying to your communication, reference (a), concerning the sinking of the White Star Liner "Republic", you are advised that this occured in 1909 off Nantucket Lightship. For your further information there is enclosed a Congressional Document, containing on page 8 an official report of this incident from the then Commanding Officer of the Revenue Cutter "Gresham", which attempted to tow the helpless steamer to safety.

     2.   As to the nature of the cargo on the "Republic" you are referred to files of any of the daily papers published at that time. As to the exact location of her sinking you can write to Captain K. W. Perry, U.S.C.G., c/o Naval District, Headquarters, 280 Broadway, New York City, as he was in command of the "Gresham" at the time of the sinking of the "Republic".

                Respectfully,

               (Signed) E. P. BERTHOLF

                    E. P. BERTHOLF,
                    Commodore Commandant.

Coast Guard Commodore-Commandant Ellsworth P. Bertholf's reply to Twentieth Century Deep Sea Salvage Syndicate's letter, February 11th, 1919. Note the curious lack of a denial: ". . . you are referred to files of any of the daily papers published at that time." *Ibid. See* Chapter Five.

Exhibit-AI

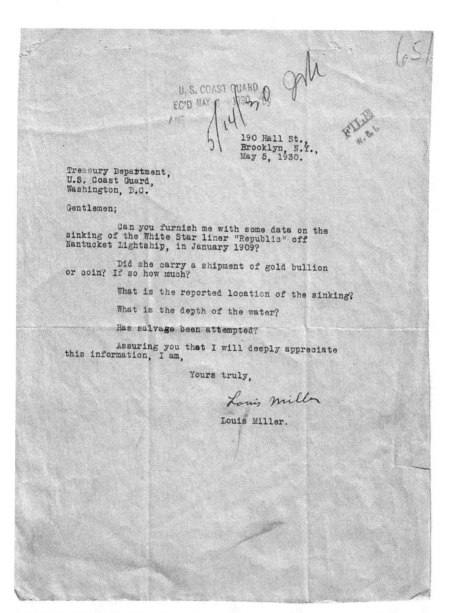

190 Hall St.,
Brooklyn, N.Y.,
May 5, 1930.

Treasury Department,
U.S. Coast Guard,
Washington, D.C.

Gentlemen;

Can you furnish me with some data on the
sinking of the White Star liner "Republic" off
Nantucket Lightship, in January 1909?

Did she carry a shipment of gold bullion
or coin? If so how much?

What is the reported location of the sinking?

What is the depth of the water?

Has salvage been attempted?

Assuring you that I will deeply appreciate
this information, I am,

Yours truly,

Louis Miller

Louis Miller.

In 1930, Mr. Miller of Brooklyn, New York, asks the Coast Guard for information on *Republic's* gold cargo. *NARA, RG 26, General Correspondence, File 651 ("RE," includes Republic).*

Exhibit-AJ

14 May, 1930.

Mr. Louis Miller,
190 Hall Street,
Brooklyn, New York.

Sir:

In reply to your letter of May 5th, in which you request to be furnished some data on the sinking of the White Star Liner REPUBLIC off Nantucket Lightship in January, 1909, I have to advise you that the records of this office show that the REPUBLIC was found by the Coast Guard Cutter GRESHAM at 5:20 p.m., Sunday, 24 January, 1909, 12.5 miles South 9° West (mag.) of Nantucket South Shoals Light Vessel and taken in tow, but sunk at 8:10 p.m., 24 January, 1909, in latitude 40°25'30" N., longitude 69°40' W., 11.7 miles S. 23° W. (mag.) from Nantucket South Shoals Light Vessel, in 40 fathoms of water.

Unofficial information at the time suggested that the REPUBLIC may have had on board $3,000,000 in American Eagles. The facts, however, are not known to this office.

From correspondence on file in this office, it appears that in the year 1909, the Deep Sea Salvage Syndicate, Marquette Building, Chicago, Illinois, was contemplating salvage operations, but it is not known by this office whether that syndicate ever undertook such operations.

Respectfully,

B. M. CHISWELL
Captain, U.S. Coast Guard,
Acting Commandant.

Captain Benjamin M. Chiswell's reply to Louis Miller, May 14th, 1930: "Unofficial information at the time suggested that the Republic may have had on board $3,000,000 in American Gold Eagles." *Ibid. See* Chapter Five.

Exhibit-AK

26835-15:8

NAVY DEPARTMENT,   S/Mn/Ls

WASHINGTON, November 12, 1914.

Gentlemen:

The receipt, through official channels,
is acknowledged of your letter of the 5th instant addressed to the general storekeeper,
navy yard, Brooklyn, in which you request information as to the value of certain naval
stores lost on the S. S. Republic in collision on January 23, 1909.

Before taking further action in the
matter it is requested that the Department be
fully advised as to the reasons that you desire the information in this instance.

Respectfully yours,

Franklin D. Roosevelt,

Acting Secretary.

The White Star Line,
No. 9 Broadway,
New York, N. Y.

Mr. G. J. Mackrell, Accountant.

Acting Secretary of the Navy Franklin D. Roosevelt's letter to White Star Line, November 12th, 1914. *NARA, RG 26, General Correspondence, File 651 ("RE," includes Republic).*

Exhibit-AL

WHITE STAR LINE

30 JAMES STREET
LIVERPOOL

CANUTE ROAD
SOUTHAMPTON

1 COCKSPUR ST., S.W.
38 LEADENHALL ST., E.C.
LONDON

NOV 16 1914

NINE BROADWAY

TELEGRAPHIC ADDRESS
"IMMERCO"

Accountants DEPARTMENT

NEW YORK   November 16th, 1914.

Franklin D. Roosevelt Esq.
Acting Secretary,
Navy Department,
Washington, D. C.

N. B.—PASSAGES ARE ONLY BOOKED SUBJECT TO ALL THE TERMS AND CONDITIONS APPEARING ON THE PASSAGE TICKETS

Dear Sir:—

We have to thank you for yours 12th, 26835- 15-8.

We beg to further explain:

Instead of making an arbitrary division of our Legal Expenses in the matter of s.s. Republic our auditors have endeavored to obtain some basis to close the different accounts.

As we have a basis for the value of the hull, baggage claims, loss in passenger fares &c., they have asked us for a basis for the value of freight shipped on the steamer.

As this is purely a matter of accountants closing this unfortunate affair we have asked you for the value for above purpose only; thus allowing us to charge to each account a proper percentage of our Attorneys expenses at New York.

Thanking you for reply, we are.

Yours truly,
Accountants Department,
White Star Line.
per

CJK/JM—

TRAVELERS CHECKS ISSUED AVAILABLE ALL OVER THE WORLD

White Star Line's response to FDR. *Ibid.*

Exhibit-AM

2d Indorsement.   26835-15:8
                    November 18, 1914.   S/Mn/Lz

From: Solicitor.
To: Bureau of Supplies and Accounts.

Subject: Letter, 11/5/14, from White Star Line requesting
          value of naval stores lost on S. S. Republic on Janu-
          ary 22, 1909.

        Returned to the Bureau with the information that the
White Star Line, under date of the 16th instant, advised
the Department as follows in respect to the purpose for
which the information in this instance was requested by
them:

            "Instead of making an arbitrary division of
        our legal expenses in the matter of S. S. Republic
        our auditors have endeavored to obtain some basis
        to close the different accounts.
            "As we have a basis for the value of the hull,
        baggage claims, loss in passenger fares, etc., they
        have asked us for the basis for the value of the
        freight shipments on the steamer.
            "As this is purely a matter of accountants'
        closing this unfortunate affair, we again ask you
        for the value for the above purpose only, thus al-
        lowing us to charge to each account a proper per-
        centage of our attorneys' expenses at New York."

        In view of the explanation furnished in this instance
this office is of the opinion that there is no objection whatever to the Bureau furnishing the White Star Line with the information requested by them.

        The files of the Department show that in the settle-
ment of this matter the naval stores lost on the Republic
were valued at $61,191.83 and that the Government received
on account of its loss in this instance the sum of $25,658.23.

                                    Graham Egerton.

                    - - - - -

The Navy's reply to White Star, November 18th, 1914. Graham Egerton was Navy lawyer,
notice the phrasing he used: "The files of the department show that in the settlement
of the matter..." *NARA, RG 26, General Correspondence, File 651 ("RE," includes Republic).*
This doesn't exactly answer the question as to what was lost. Was that intentional? *See*
Chapter Six.

Exhibit-AN

If the $3 million loan really was for the Russians, proof might include disbursement orders from the Russian State Bank to French banks involved in the French-Russian loan in the amount of $3 million. Here are, perhaps, two of them. Five million Francs was roughly equivalent to $1 million. Does another disbursement order exist for the third million?

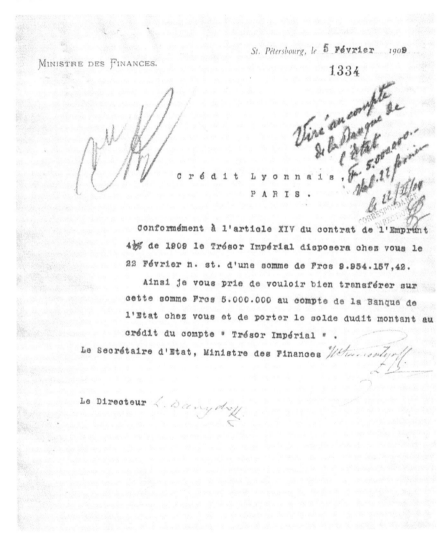

Disbursement order from Crédit Lyonnais' archives directing $1,000,000 (5 million Francs) to go to the Russian State Bank on February 22nd. *Ibid. See* Chapter Eight.

Notice the documents numbering: 1334 and 1335. Somewhere out there is either 1333 or 1336, the final instruction to pay the Russian State Bank on February 22nd. Discovering these documents in the private archives confirmed my belief of the commercial Russian State Bank as the mystery borrower, and the rumors that this gold shipment was, and is, on *Republic*.

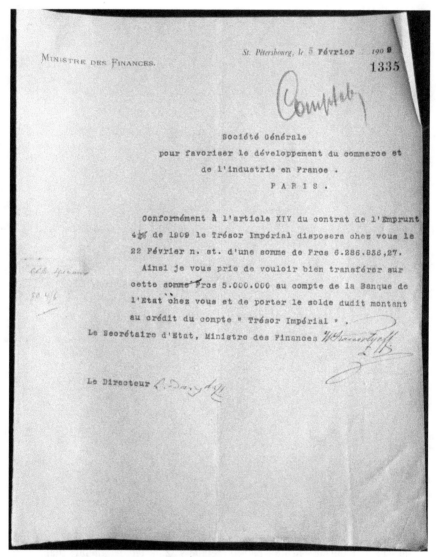

Disbursement order from Société Générale's archives directing $1 million (5 million Francs) to go to the Russian State Bank on February 22nd. *See* Chapter Eight.

Exhibit-AP

THE RESOLUTION

When I discovered *Republic* in 1981, she was pristine. The only major salvage efforts occurred later in 1986 and 1987, and both failed to locate the part of the wreck that would contain the gold. Some photos of the '87 effort and subsequent expeditions are below.

Our Diving Support Vessel (DSV) for the 1987 effort, the *SOSI Inspector*, waits ready to begin salvaging.

Dropping a one-man submarine off the side of the *Inspector*.

Pulling up one of *Republic*'s 14,000-lb anchors. The anchors are currently on loan and rest outside the Fall River Maritime Museum in Fall River, MA.

A crewmember uncovering a White Star plate from 3rd Class/Steerage.

Republic's aft helm, marked "A345," that we salvaged. It now rests snugly in the corner of my dining room.

We recovered hundreds of bottles of wine and champagne from the wreck when we excavated deep into the ship in '87. We didn't have access then to the quantity and quality of information about the cargoes that we have today, and that you will discover for yourself within this book.

Top: S.S. *Republic* – GROUP OF 66 WINE BOTTLES – These bottles are full and still sealed. They contain wine and some are currently being tested to see if they are still drinkable.

We've made many expeditions to *Republic* since 1987, with recent trips for conducting surveys of the wrecksite and pinpointing our target areas. We are gearing up for our next major recovery effort, an effort that will finally bring this 100-year old mystery to an exciting, and I think very prosperous conclusion.

UNITED STATES DISTRICT COURT
FOR THE DISTRICT OF MASSACHUSETTS

CIVIL ACTION
NO. 00-11565 (NG)
MARTHA'S VINEYARD SCUBA HEADQUARTERS INC.   (Consld. 82-3742)

Plaintiff,

v.

THE WRECKED AND ABANDONED STEAM VESSEL
R.M.S. REPUBLIC, her tackle, apparel and cargo, etc.
located within 2,000 yards of a point: Beginning at coordinates
40 degrees 26 minutes 00 seconds N. Latitude and 69 degrees
46 minutes 00 seconds W. Longitude; more precisely Loran "C"
coordinates 25138.1, 43453.2 through .6 and 14073.1, .2, *in rem,*

Defendant.

**Order Granting Plaintiff MVSHQ, Inc.'s Motion For Judgment *In Rem* Awarding
Good and Legal Title In Regard to the Defendant Vessel R.M.S. REPUBLIC,
including her tackle, apparel, appurtenances, and cargo, etc. to MVSHQ, Inc.**

UPON DUE CONSIDERATION of Plaintiff, MARTHA'S VINEYARD SCUBA
HEADQUARTERS, INC.'s ("MVSHQ") supplemental motion filed August 5, 2011 by its
attorneys, before this Court and all papers in connection therewith and in opposition thereto, if
any, as well as the record of the hearing convened August 3, 2011 in regard to other related
pending motions brought by Plaintiff that have also been considered by this Court, and for good
cause shown:

IT IS ORDERED AND ADJUDGED that

(1) the Defendant Vessel R.M.S. REPUBLIC and all her tackle, apparel, appurtenances,
and cargo , that also includes the personal effects of all others, such as officers, crew
members and passengers, contained within the wreck site area at the coordinates
previously pleaded herein, (hereinafter referred to as "Defendant Vessel and her

The first page of the court order awarding legal title of RMS *Republic* and her cargoes to
MVSHQ, Inc. The result of nearly three decades of litigation.

Exhibit-AT

From the 1981 expedition on the *Wahoo* to search for *Republic*, taken at the dock that ran between my shop and The Black Dog on Martha's Vineyard. From left: Joe Martino, Norman Gardner, a younger (and thinner) version of me, Kent Guernsey, Janet Bieser, John Farrington, and Hank Keats. From right: Capt. Steve Bielenda, Doug Campbell.

From a trip to the wreck in 2005 on *Sea Hunter*. From left: Tim Barrow, me, Vladamir Goravatski, Mark Silverstein, John Bricker, Wes Carmen, Kevin Dorman, Grant Bayerle, Norman Gardner. This was my son Grant's first trip to the *Republic*.

Exhibit-AU

CHAPTER EIGHT

The Tsar's Secret

"What's going to happen to me and all of Russia?"

— Tsar Nicholas II

It would be called the first great war of the 20th century, and it would foreshadow a much greater one. To anyone paying attention, the Russo-Japanese War of 1904-1905 would reveal hints of warfare to come: machine guns and trenches and ground-shaking artillery. It was brutal, it was bloody, and it was expensive. For Russia and Tsar Nicholas II, it was a disaster. And an early sign of the end.

Russia had been encroaching on Manchuria and Korea since the end of the Sino-Japanese War in 1895, the results of which had increased Japan's sphere of influence over both regions, previously the dominions of China. Russia had leased Port

Arthur (now Lushun), resting on the southern tip of Manchuria's Liaodong Peninsula. It was their one warm water port, a geographic and political necessity for the Tsar. But little by little, the Russians had begun making their presence felt more and more throughout the whole region. And making Japan nervous in the process.

As Russia increased her foray into the new Japanese territory, Japan began flexing her muscles as well. First by negotiation and diplomacy. When those failed, Japan struck militarily. On February 8th, 1904 the Japanese Imperial Navy attacked the Russian Far East Fleet at Port Arthur, sinking *Tsessarevitch* and *Retvizan*, two of Russia's finest battleships, along with *Pallada*, a valued cruiser. The attack shocked the Tsar who had been advised by his ministers that Japan was unprepared for war and not at all likely to want to engage in it with the Russians. As badly as the ministers underestimated the military capabilities of Japan is as badly as Nicholas overestimated his own military. But others did, too. After war was declared between the two powers, the western world was stunned as Japan emerged victorious in battle after battle.

When the war ended in September of '05, with a peace treaty brokered by none other than Teddy Roosevelt (for which he was awarded the Nobel Peace Prize), Russia had been chased out of Manchuria as well as Korea. The Tsar was politically wounded at home and abroad. And to add insult to injury, Russia was also now millions of dollars in debt.

It was the latest in a series of ill-fated affairs for the Tsar. Coming to power in 1894 at just 26 years old, after the unexpected death of his father, Alexander III, Nicholas was, by many accounts, unprepared for his role as leader of a land as vast and diverse as the Russian empire. Upon his ascension to Tsar, he is reported to have asked his cousin with no small amount of trepidation, "What's going to happen to me and all of Russia?"[76] His reign even started ominously, with a stampede on Khodynka Field in Moscow following his official coronation. Promised gifts in celebration, including free beer and pretzels, close to half a million people turned out. When rumors began to swirl that there would not be enough beer and pretzels for everyone, the crowd rushed forward creating a panic. Over 1,300 people were trampled to death. Now, with the loss of the war, a collapsing economy, and threats of revolution, Nicholas's rule wasn't getting any better.

Most of Nicholas's debt was to France, $160 million for monies borrowed to fight the Japanese. France was Russia's ally at a time when seemingly every country in Europe was allied with at least one other. Since Otto Von Bismarck's Germany rose to military prominence with its victory over the French in the Franco-Prussian War of 1870-'71, all of Europe had been made wary. Germany, a loose confederation of states before Bismarck, was

---

[76] Feinstein, Elaine. *Anna of All the Russians*, NY, NY: Vintage, 2006.

now a power to be feared. France to Germany's west allied with Russia on Germany's east. Britain, fearing a German attack from the Channel, allied with Belgium and France. Serbia was allied with Russia. Germany, for her part, was allied with the Austro-Hungarian Empire. It was, of course, a tinderbox that needed little more than the assassination of an Austrian archduke in Bosnia to serve as the match. The ensuing conflagration, begun in 1914, would become known as The Great War until an even greater one would come along and impose a name change: World War I.

In 1905, European war was several years off but the threat was real and France had determined it was in her political interest to keep Russia solvent. That political position only intensified after Russia's loss to Japan. If you owe someone a little, goes the old saying, you have a creditor; if you owe someone a lot, you have a partner. The French loan, due in May of 1909, was renegotiated. Russia would get a new loan – $160 million to pay off the old loan and an additional $90 million to keep the Tsar afloat, much of which was needed immediately to satisfy Russia's 1909 budgetary requirements. The loan closed on January 22, 1909. An interesting date. *Republic*, it might be remembered, sailed from New York the very same day.

THE RUSSIAN LOANS
1904-1909 LOAN SCHEDULE

1904 - 5-YEAR $160 MILLION LOAN
(TO FINANCE WAR WITH JAPAN)

SINGLE BALLOON-PAYMENT DUE MAY 1909

$160 MM

1904   May 1909

1909 - 50-YEAR $240 MILLION LOAN
(TO PAY-OFF 1904 LOAN AND 1909 BUDGET DEFICIT)

AMORTIZED OVER 50 YEARS

$240 MM

Jan. 22, 1909   1959

$240 MILLION LOAN DISTRIBUTION

1904 $160 MM Loan Repayment

Loan Closed   20%   20%   15%   15%   15%   15%

Jan. 22   Feb. 22   Mar. 22   Apr. 22   May 22   Jun. 22   Jul. 22

MYSTERIOUS $3,000,000 30-DAY SHORT-TERM LOAN
(PROCURED IN NEW YORK. AT A BELOW-MARKET RATE)

Loan Closes   Repayment
"Republic" Departs   of Loan

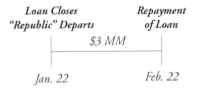

$3 MM

Jan. 22   Feb. 22

The $90 million was to be parceled out by French banks over six months. Six French banks underwrote the loan. A British bank, a Dutch bank, and other subsidiary players were involved as well. Twenty percent of the $90 million was to be released on February 22nd, 20% on March 22nd, and 15% on the 22nd of each of the following four months, through July. What that meant initially was that the Tsar would have to wait an entire month after the loan closed before he received the first installment.

But if Russia couldn't meet her 1909 budget obligations, she would have needed money sooner. And this theory would explain a very interesting transaction that was first reported in New York on January 15th, 1909, a transaction with a very interesting number attached to it: $3 million. The parties to the transaction, a short-term loan, remained a mystery. This is how it was described by the *New York Tribune* the following day: "A loan of $3,000,000 at 1-½ per cent for thirty days was reported in Wall Street yesterday and was said to mark a new record for time money loans."[77] All the other papers reported it, too. The low rate only added to the mystery. The *New York Times* reported that, "Money brokers were unable to recall any cheaper rate for this period. The lowest recorded quotation for thirty-day money was 2-½ per cent in 1904."[78]

Worthy of note is the arrival of a certain visitor to New York and the timing of the visit. Russia's financial agent, Gregory

---

[77] *New York Tribune*, "Big Time Loan at 1-1/2 Reported", January 16th, 1909, p. 11.
[78] *New York Times*, "Low Rate for Money Loans", January 16th, 1909, p. 14:2.

113

Wilenkin, showed up in New York, according to Ellis Island records, on January 14th, the day before the $3 million short-term mystery loan was first reported. More interesting still is the timing of his departure: he left New York January 23rd, the day after *Republic* set sail.

The size of the short-term loan (close to 80 million in today's dollars based on purchasing power) and at such a low interest rate narrows the identity of the mystery borrower considerably. Only an entity as substantial as a sovereign government could borrow such money. And even at that, a New York bank (or perhaps banks) wouldn't lend such a sum, and at such a low rate, unless it was practically risk-free. And Russia, as everyone knew, was due to get their first installment of their French loan – $18,000,000 – some thirty days later. (Exactly 30 days, in fact, from the sailing of *Republic*.)

But of course even such a risk-free loan would certainly warrant a market rate. Banks are in business to make money, after all. But there is more than one way to make a loan profitable. A loan to Russia, paid off in thirty days by, essentially, French banks, would effectively result in a free exchange of dollars for European currency. The lending New York bank (or banks) would then have foreign monies available, Francs perhaps, that they could sell for a profit to their New York clients, clients who had to make payments within France.

For her part, Russia needed gold. Liquidity of real value.

Her 1909 loan from the French had been under negotiation since early 1906. *The Commercial and Financial Chronicle* in January of 1909 described the difficulties: "[The loan] was inevitably postponed, first, on account of the great strain then existing on the whole world's money markets [in 1906]; again, in 1907, because of the well-known panic conditions throughout the financial world. Efforts were made on two or three occasions during 1908 to bring the matter to a head, but were defeated through [recent unrest in the Balkan states]."[79] After the loan eventually closed and after the sinking of *Republic*, Eduard Netzlin, lead negotiator for the French banking consortium of the loan, would write to V.N. Kokovtsov, Russia's Minister of Finance, summing up the experience: "I hope that my information will give the same satisfaction to your Excellency and you will be willing to recognize that it was uneasy to guide this operation via all the underwater rocks it was facing on its way."[80] Interesting choice of metaphor.

In any event, by the time the loan had finally closed, it's reasonable to assume that the Tsar's coffers were under a significant strain. And Russia was well into its 1909 budget year. And there was still a month remaining between the closing of the French loan and the first installment. A 30-day interim loan does not seem unlikely.

---

[79] *Commercial and Financial Chronicle*, January, 1909, p. 128:2.

[80] Arkiv, Krasnyi, *The Correspondence between V.N. Kokovstov and Eduard Netzlin (1906-1909)*, 4:131-156.

And the likely place to get it would have been the U.S., specifically New York. With a favorable exchange rate and seemingly unending supply, New York was where the world went for gold. As *Bankers Magazine* put it in their April, 1909 issue, "Should the Timarch of Timbuktu desire to buy new hats for his wives, he would doubtless ask Uncle Sam to fork over a few millions in Eagles."[81] And after all, New York is where France itself went to get a goodly portion of the gold it had planned on disbursing to the Russian Treasury Department on February 22nd. "New York's Gold to Help Russian Loan," read the headline in the January 13th *New York Evening Mail*. "The shipments of gold from New York are destined for the Bank of France. The movement is a natural one resulting from the favorable exchange rate."

One likely lending source in particular might have been the Guaranty Trust Company of New York. Max May, Vice President of the bank, was widely considered to be unequaled in foreign exchange. May built up Guaranty's foreign exchange business to "astonishingly large proportions," reported the *New York Times*, summarizing his tenure in a 1918 article; "his daily transactions having averaged as high as $20,000,000 a day. His total turnover in busy years has amounted to more than $6,000,000,000 – a total not approached by any banking institution in the country."[82] And May was not unfamiliar with Russia in particular, going

---

[81] *Bankers Magazine*, April, 1909.

[82] *New York Times*, "Max May Retires for Period of War", January 10th, 1918.

on to become a director and member of the board of the Russian Commercial Bank of Moscow in 1922.

For the Tsar's part, an advantageous interest rate of 1-½% on the loan would have been made even more attractive by the fact that France was paying Russia 1-¼% for the 30 days that they were holding the first installment of $18 million. If Russia had an immediate need for gold, it would have bordered on financial irresponsibility *not* to have borrowed it from New York, if such favorable terms were available. And we know by the news reports that those terms were, indeed, available to someone.

Did Gregory Wilenkin, Russian financial agent, represent the mystery borrower? Forty-five years old, Wilenkin was attached to the Russian embassy in Washington, D.C. where he had been since May of 1904. As a Russian Jew, he had presumably been sent to the U.S. as financial agent in order to better develop Russia's connections and influence with prominent Jewish principals of New York's banking industry. And he had been successful, making "a most favorable impression," reported the *Jewish Chronicle* in September of 1905.[83]

Working directly under Sergei Yulyevich Witte, Russian Minister of Finance, Wilenkin was instrumental in the acquisition of the $160 million loan from France during the war in 1904. Too, he had intimate knowledge of the Treaty of Portsmouth, the treaty

---

[83] *Jewish Chronicle*, September 1st, 1905, p. 10.

brokered by Roosevelt to end the war. Witte had been called upon by the Tsar himself to negotiate for Russia, his efforts earning him the title of Count. Wilenkin was his secretary/advisor.

For his visit to New York, Wilenkin applied for and received diplomatic credentials from the U.S. State Department. This seems odd. According to accounts of his trip to New York in the social sections of the daily newspapers, it was one of pleasure, not business. He was reportedly on leave from his duties, had brought along his wife, stayed at the St. Regis Hotel, and, according to the January 23rd *New York Herald*, "He and Mme. Wilenkin have been entertained a great deal while they have been in New York." From there it was on to San Francisco, Honolulu, and eventually Tokyo ("The relations between Russia and Japan are now of the most friendly nature," he had explained to the *Herald*). The story was that Wilenkin was most likely going to take a permanent post in Japan. But less than a year later, Wilenkin was back in the States, still acting in the capacity of the financial agent of the Imperial Russian Government.

Was the vacation story a ruse? Diplomatic status might have been a necessity if the trip to New York wasn't quite the holiday it was projected to be. Wilenkin would have needed it in order to obligate the Russian State Bank in a foreign loan. That he sought diplomatic status is eyebrow-raising enough. More interesting still is that Wilenkin's status came with an exemption from having to have his luggage inspected. A special letter from the U.S. Treasury Department dated January 14[84], 1909 confirmed

that instructions were sent to the Collector of Customs in New

York directing him "to extend the usual courtesies, including the

free entry of his baggage, to Mr. Wilenkin, Commercial Attaché."[84]

Not that there may have been anything out of the ordinary in

his luggage upon arrival in New York. But the exemption would

certainly have gone a long way towards keeping questions to a

minimum regarding anything loaded aboard *Republic* with the

name Gregory Wilenkin attached to it.[85]

If Russia borrowed $3 million for thirty days from New

York, one might hope that, in terms of evidence, there may be

separate disbursement orders somewhere from Russia to the

participating French banks, making arrangements specifically for

$3 million of the $18 million due to the Russians on February 22nd

to be released so that Russia could pay her short-term New York

creditors. Through painstaking, needle-in-haystack research, I

found two such disbursement orders in two French bank archives.

One is addressed to the bank Crédit Lyonnais and the other to

the bank Société Générale. Both are from the Russian Ministry of

Finance and are worded almost identically. The letters request the

---

[84] *See* Photos & Exhibits, Exhibit-V.

[85] Interestingly, Wilenkin was connected by marriage to the London branch of Seligman Brothers (*The Reform Advocate*, May 14th, 1910, p.1), the London fiscal agent for the U.S. Navy. This relationship becomes more interesting in light of the missing Navy payroll and more interesting still when Seligman's relationship with Louis Hirsch and Company is considered. Hirsch was a Paris banking concern that shipped, at least in part, the gold aboard *Oceanic*. Wilenkin, it seems, knew all the right people in all the right places.

banks, upon disbursement of the February 22nd loan, to "be kind enough to transfer the sum of 5,000,000 Francs to the [Russian] State Bank."[86]

Two points here. First, five million Francs in February, 1909 were worth roughly one million dollars. The two disbursement orders, then, would account for two thirds of the short-term loan. Since several banks were involved in disbursing the loan proceeds, and with each French bank holding only its share of 1909 bond receipts that it had committed to sell, but with no one bank holding an amount of bond proceeds sufficient to disburse the entire $3 million on February 22, it's reasonable to imagine that there might be a third disbursement order for another five million Francs hidden away in a third bank's archives. Second, this possibility is made more likely by the nature of these two disbursement orders. Both instruct that the money go to the Russian State Bank. What's noteworthy about this is that every other disbursement instruction having to do with France's big loan to Russia required that the loan proceeds be sent to the Russian Treasury Department, not the State Bank. But it would be the State Bank, not the Treasury Department, that would enter into a short-term loan, such as a $3 million loan from New York. The State Bank was Russia's foreign exchange bank, after all. And it was the State Bank that was reported to have received a short-term loan from

---

[86] *See* Photos & Exhibits, Exhibit-AO and Exhibit-AP.

France of $10 million back in '06 when France and Russia were beginning the thorny negotiations of the long-term $160 million loan ("All the French Bankers Will Do Is To Make Short-Term Advances," read the subheading in a *New York Times* article from January 7, 1906). It would be the State Bank, then, that would pay back the New York banks. It would be the Russian State Bank that would have immediate need of $3 million of the $18 million disbursed on February 22nd.

A few facts to pull all of this together. Since the sinking of *Republic* there have been rumors of lost gold, $3 million being the number most associated with the rumors. A "mystery loan" of $3 million was procured in New York on January 15th, 1909, the day after Russia's financial agent, Gregory Wilenkin, arrived in New York. *Republic* sailed from New York on January 22nd. Wilenkin left New York on January 23rd. Russia had an urgent need for funds, and a 30-day loan at a favorable rate (almost free when taking into account the interest France was paying Russia for those thirty days) would have been too perfect to pass up. And it would have carried Russia to February 22nd, the date of the first disbursement from the French. Two disbursement orders for $1 million each from the Russian State Bank have been uncovered in the archives of French banks. A third might exist, or it might have been lost to history.

On top of all of that, there is this: the French loan to Russia closed on January 22nd although it was originally scheduled to close the day before. Cunard's *Carmania*, it might be remembered, was scheduled to leave New York on January 21st, originally planning to ship the Navy provisions for the Great White Fleet. But then the plans changed and *Republic* became the ship of transport for the fleet, sailing one day later than *Carmania*. Why the change from *Carmania*? Is it possible that Russia required the increased security inherent in a ship delivering Navy goods? But the New York loan would certainly have had as a condition the successful closing of the French loan. Since that was delayed a day, it seems at least possible that *Republic* was then chosen to deliver the fleet provisions to appease the Russian security concerns. *Carmania* had left by the time the French loan closed, but *Republic* was available. It's hard to believe these events are unconnected: the loan was originally scheduled to close on January 21st and *Carmania* was originally scheduled to ship the Navy provisions on January 21st; instead, the loan closed on January 22nd, and it was decided that *Republic* would ship the Navy provisions on January 22nd. The timing is too coincidental to dismiss. Not just the dates, but even down to the hour. The loan would have closed no later than 5:00 p.m. Paris time, 11:00 a.m. New York time (probably even earlier, with European banker's hours). And *Republic* wasn't scheduled to leave New York until 3:00 p.m. And so there was time. Not a lot, but Russia would have wanted to move quickly. Interest was accruing and the Tsar needed the gold. *Republic* became the ideal transport, leaving nearly immediately after the loan closed, and

– it must be noted – the only liner leaving New York for Europe that day.

As for the actual delivery of the gold, at least a couple options present themselves. Several countries sent ships to greet the American fleet in Gibraltar, *Republic*'s destination. Russia, as it turns out, had her Baltic fleet (the remnants anyway, since the war) in attendance. The *Boston Journal* of February 1st described the scene: On the arrival of the American fleet, "the Russian battleships *Tsarevitch* and *Slava*, and the protected cruisers *Bogatyr* and *Oleg*, and the French gunboat *Cassini*, and the Dutch gunboat *Heindall*, lying inside the breakwater, with sides manned, flags dipping and bands playing, greeted the Americans as each in turn entered and was berthed. The American battleships responded with flags and music, the band on board the *Connecticut* playing the national anthem of each country represented. As they passed the Russian warships …the American bands rendered 'God Save the Czar.'"[87] Nothing less than battleships would provide the security Russia no doubt felt it needed to transport from Gibraltar a Tsar's fortune in gold.

The straightest route would have been through the Mediterranean, the Turkish controlled Dardanelles and Bosporus straits, and into the Black Sea from where Russia's southernmost ports could be accessed. However, by an 1841 agreement

---

[87] *Boston Journal*, February 1st, 1909, p. 12:1.

between England, France, Russia, Austria, and Prussia (reaffirmed in 1856 by the Congress of Paris at the end of the Crimean War), the Bosporus and Dardanelles straits were closed in peacetime to all warships except Turkish warships, a convention that would remain in effect until World War I.

More than likely then, the Russian warships, equipped with ice-breaking bows, would have sailed the gold through any one of several Russian Baltic Fleet naval bases, including the base at Kronstadt, a satellite town of St. Petersburg located on Kotlin island in the Gulf of Finland, a mere 18 miles from the Tsar's capital. Or perhaps to the normally ice-free naval base at Reval (Tallinn in today's Estonia), at the mouth of the Gulf of Finland and 230 miles from St. Petersburg. There was also the ice-free naval base at Libau (Liepaja in today's Latvia), 560 miles from St. Petersburg. And there were other ports, any one of which could provide rail access to the Tsar's Winter Palace.

To add more intrigue to the mix, it's entirely possible, though no direct evidence has yet appeared, that the $3 million might well have been only a part of the Russian shipment aboard *Republic*. It's likely Russia had reserves in the New York banks to begin with. If the Tsar was in need of money urgently, why stop at $3 million? If you're in New York borrowing money, why not take your own money as well? If Wilenkin pulled Russia's reserves from New York, that would have added to the shipment significantly. It's also possible he borrowed more than $3 million. Maybe much more. That a single $3 million short-term loan was leaked to the press might be more than serendipity for someone research-ing the possible sources of gold aboard *Republic*; it might also be the tip of the iceberg. And let's not forget that France herself was amassing gold from New York for the Russian loan. Might France have had gold on board, too?

The fact is, secret transactions were not uncommon. In September of 1905, just after the signing of the Treaty of Portsmouth, the staggering sum of $22 million was shipped from the United States to Paris with barely anyone noticing. An im-port/export analysis of gold movement at that time reveals this.[88] And a *Wall Street Journal* article from August 29th, 1905 hints at it and suggests the reason: "The first result expected [from the peace conference] is that Japan would withdraw to Europe money now on deposit in New York...Persons with good opportunities for judging estimates of the amount of money now on deposit in New York to the credit of the Japanese government say it does not exceed $20,000,000 to $25,000,000." Such a huge amount leaving the U.S. market might have created a panic. But Treasury Secretary L.M. Shaw, according to the *Journal* on September 2nd, assured that New York banks, financing the large sum, were recalling their short-term notes to cover an "unusual August demand for crop money." A much more likely reason, given the timing, was Japan's

---

[88] *See* Appendix, Exhibit III.

desire to enter the Paris financial market after the war. It's not outside of the realm of possibility to imagine that such a condition was part of the treaty. Part of the negotiations might even have included a sub rosa payment from Japan to the Tsar. Compensation for abnegating his warm water port? Russia's was not an unconditional surrender. There was a reason, after all, that Finance Minister Sergei Yulyevich Witte arrived at the negotiating table as a minister and left as a count.

The point is simple and unsurprising: governments are not above concealing the shipments of politically sensitive cargoes. We can look at all the circumstances and determine that $3 million was likely aboard, but we can at least speculate that more, perhaps much more, was aboard as well.

Either way, the fact is if a significant amount of gold was headed to Russia but lost on board *Republic*, it would have been in everyone's best interest – Russia, France, Japan, the United States, as well as Great Britain (France's ally) – to keep the loss concealed. The revelation of the short-term loan borrower, if indeed Russia, would have exposed the precariousness of the Tsar's financial condition. Bondholders in Europe might well have panicked. The Russian government itself might have collapsed, eight years before it, in fact, did. Propping up the Tsar was a political necessity for France as well as for the stability of an already-teetering Europe. War was closing in. And the loan would have called even more public attention to the nature of the alliance, thus vexing

126

Germany and Austria in the process. And the loss itself, notwith-standing the tremendous political ramifications had it become public knowledge, could have thrown the world financial markets into uncertain turmoil.

The combination of Russia's shaky financial condition and her alliance with France (and by extension Great Britain) cannot be underestimated with respect to historical importance. Undercurrents of the revolution that would ultimately topple the Tsar were, by 1909, becoming apparent. Already Nicholas had been forced to cede some of his autocratic power to a parliament that had been established in 1906 – that in response to riotous political and social unrest throughout all of Russia. The workers of the Russian world were beginning to unite, finding voice in an ex-iled Vladimir Ilyich Lenin. The loss of Russia to revolution would mean grave consequences for France. If Germany had no serious threat from her east, it would mean she could concentrate all of her forces to her west, overrunning Belgium and France in short order and establishing a valuable, dangerous, launching point for a naval invasion of England. As it played out, the Russian revolu-tion was delayed, taking place three years into World War I, caus-ing Germany to split her forces and get hopelessly bogged down in the trenches of France.

And now we know what Winston Churchill, President of the British Board of Trade, knew and why he kept it a secret, why there was no British inquiry made into the sinking of *Republic*, or why, if an inquiry was held, the findings were kept out of public view. Since there was no inquiry held in the United States either, it's a safe bet that Nobel Prize-winning Teddy Roosevelt, with unparalleled access to the true Russian financial picture having brokered the terms of peace with Japan, would have known, too.

Roosevelt's concealment of the loss would be consistent with his (now) known *secret du roi* style of diplomacy. Edmund Morris presents an instructive example in his Pulitzer Prize bestseller *Theodore Rex* (Random House). Describing Roosevelt's actions in what has become known as the "Venezuela Crisis" of 1903, Morris writes:

> The full extent of the crisis would have to be inferred circumstantially, from an extraordinary void in the archives of three nations – deletion after deletion hinting at some vanished enormity, a painted-out battle of Titans visible in pentimento through layers of pale wash.[89]

It was common for Roosevelt to keep politically sensitive matters from the press and off the official record. Through "defoliation" of sensitive records by loyal archivists on both sides of the Atlantic, the Venezuelan crisis was designed to fade from public consciousness.[90] In fact, in his annual address to Congress in December of 1902, despite the underlying diplomatic crisis and potential war with Germany, Roosevelt stated that there was "not

---

[89] Morris, Edmund, *Theodore Rex*, NY, NY: Random House, 2001, p. 177.
[90] Ibid, p. 210.

a cloud on the horizon at present ... not the slightest chance of trouble with a foreign power."[91] *Not a cloud on the horizon*. A coincidence *worthy of mention*. Roosevelt's words are nothing if not intriguing.

The loss of a politically sensitive gold cargo would have resulted in congruent methods of secrecy. Probably offset by a captive private insurer, the $3 million loss, the Tsar's gold, remained beneath the surface. For years. Until now. What's left is to take a closer look at where the treasure might today be. Let's follow the trail to where it naturally leads, to the last place the gold might have been seen by human eyes – on board *Republic*, now off the coast of Nantucket, 40 fathoms below the surface.

---

[91] Marks III, Frederick W., *Velvet on Iron*, University of Nebraska Press, 1979, p. 52.

CHAPTER NINE

Salvage

"O cursed lust for gold,
To what dost thou not drive the hearts of men?"

— Virgil

Twelve hours after *Florida* and *Republic* collided, Thomas Fenlon of Standard Oil's cargo ship *City of Everett* asked *Republic's* Captain Inman Sealby if Sealby might be interested in making use of *City of Everett's* accompanying 6,000-ton capacity barge, or Fenlon's pumps, capable of drawing two-million gallons of water an hour. Sealby brusquely declined Fenlon's offers. Eventually, the two main ships providing assistance to *Republic* would be *Gresham* and *Seneca*. Sealby's choice of help was probably not random. *Gresham* and *Seneca* were both United States Revenue Cutters. *City of Everett* was privately owned.

The difference is significant. Both *Gresham* and *Seneca* were obligated by official government duty to render aid. *City of Everett*, on the other hand, was under no such obligation. Fenlon's offer was voluntarily made. This would satisfy one of three conditions that were no doubt important to Fenlon. Together with the other two conditions – *Republic* was in peril, and *City of Everett*'s efforts may well have saved her or at least some of her property – Standard Oil would have been within its legal rights to expect a salvage award, perhaps a large one.

Salvage law goes back centuries, with its roots in antiquity. The cornerstone principle of the law is that the successful efforts of a salvor who has voluntarily risked his life and property to save lives, ships, and the property of others imperiled at sea ought to be amply rewarded. Salvage reached a zenith in the seventeenth and eighteenth centuries as a whole cottage industry sprang from the idea, with "wreckers" making good livings (albeit risky ones) coming to the rescue of ships sailing into reefs throughout the Caribbean. In the United States, the industry hit its stride in the 1800s, in New England but also notably throughout the Florida Keys. Key West, surrounded by perilous reefs, became a rich boomtown from salvage alone.

With *Republic* sunk, there was, of course, nothing upon which to lay a salvage claim even if a private ship had come to her rescue. Not so the *Florida* which managed to limp into port. And in fact three tugboat operators filed suit against *Florida*, alleging,

reported the *New York Times* on January 30th, 1909, "that the services of their tugboats were valuable and that…they are entitled to
liberal salvage."

A ship is under no obligation to accept help, of course, and
Sealby's refusal of Fenlon's offer ensured that there would be no
future salvage claims from Standard Oil. It also meant a roll of
the dice for Sealby. One refuses help at one's own risk. There's no
way to know what Fenlon's barge and pumps could have done for
Republic, but we know what happened without them. For his part,
Sealby believed *Republic* would stay afloat at least long enough to
be towed in, her cargo intact. As captain with final authority, he
was nevertheless in contact via wireless with White Star officials.
Sealby's refusals of help might well have been ordered by his su-
periors from their New York offices.

Thomas Fenlon's offer, as it happens, was not the only one.
The *New York, Lucania*, and the *Furnessia* – all private ships – offered assistance. The wireless operators of *New York* and *Lucania*
told the *New York Times* they were certain that "the *Republic* could
have been saved had Captain Sealby accepted the proffers of aid
made to him by the captains of the ships that surrounded him."
The January 26th, 1909 *Times* article continued: "…shortly after
the *New York* found the *Republic*…Capt. Roberts of the *New York*
shouted through his megaphone to Capt. Sealby that shallow water was only a few miles distant, and that he would willingly tow
the *Republic* where she could be beached if Capt. Sealby so wished.

According to Allen, Capt. Sealby shouted back that he intended to wait for the tugs that were being rushed to him by the White Star Line, and that he would have to decline all offers of aid."[92]

Furnessia, as it turned out, an Anchor Line ship, did, in fact, ultimately assist with the towing. Perhaps White Star officials contacted, and negotiated with, Anchor Line officials. Maybe no such communication had taken place between White Star and Standard Oil. Either way, by then it was too late. White Star's calculated gamble meant the end for *Republic*, a $1.5 million loss. But it didn't necessarily mean the end for her cargo – $3.8 million (that we know about), more than twice the amount of the ship's worth.

One question that has often presented itself: given the time that *Republic* stayed afloat – 39 hours –, were any salvage attempts made upon the cargo itself? The fact is, after *Baltic* – a sister White Star liner – steamed into the area finding *Republic* still afloat, it would be an additional four hours before she would make her way over to *Florida* to begin that painstaking passenger transfer. James Connolly wrote about it in *Colliers*: "[*Baltic*] did not stay with us [on *Florida*]. No, she steamed back to the side of the *Republic* and there remained, looking after her company's property no doubt – all very well at any other time, but here were fifteen hundred souls who could not see why they were not taken off while the sea was smooth, the air dry and the sky alight with

---

[92] *New York Times*, January 26th, 1909, p. 4:5.

encouraging stars…At about eleven o'clock the *Baltic* did come near, the word was passed to get ready to leave…but now it was foggy and rainy, and the rising sea not so smooth…Those four hours during which *Baltic* remained away – looking after company property – seemed a terrible waste of time to those aboard the *Florida*."[93]

But although precious little information exists from crew accounts and official reports as to just what occurred during that four hour period, it seems highly unlikely, given the circumstances, that any of *Republic*'s cargo, in particular her gold cargo, could have made its way off the ship. Gold is extraordinarily heavy. Two years earlier, *Lusitania* sailed into New York with a cargo of gold and the offloading was described by a *New York Times* report like so: "A gang of longshoremen rushed up the freight gangplank and tackled the piles of small wooden boxes. It took two men to drag each box down the gangway to the pier…the longshoremen perspired under their loads… impressed with the weight of the boxes."[94] To imagine that a skeleton crew, concerned with keeping a ship afloat, could conceivably carry similarly heavy boxes of gold coins down the accommodation ladder of a poorly-lighted, sinking ship, into small boats, across a few hundred feet of open ocean and up another ladder (maybe even a rope ladder!) and

---

[93] James B. Connolly, "The Sinking of the 'Republic'," *Colliers*, Feb. 6th, 1909, pps. 11-12.

[94] *New York Times*, November 9th, 1907.

all without ever breathing a word about it, strains all manner of reason.

Adding to the unlikelihood is that before the crates of gold could even be offloaded, they had to be retrieved. *Republic*, like most transatlantic vessels, had a specie room, a storage locker specifically for specie – coined money. *Standard Seamanship for the Merchant Service*, a 1922 shipping manual, described such a room on the first-class passenger ship of the period: "The specie room is a strong box located near the bottom of the vessel. A good plan is to locate this room at the bottom of a trunk hatch, and after the specie is on board fill the hatch with the baggage not wanted on voyage. This makes it impossible to get at the treasure without hoisting out the entire cargo of baggage."[95] And with *Republic*'s power out, her winches rendered useless, hoisting could only have been accomplished manually.

And there was yet another problem. *Republic*'s specie room, located aft on the orlop deck – the lowest deck of the ship – was under water. *Republic* by then had been listing towards the stern and would, in fact, eventually go down stern first. The specie room was flooded; the sea was already laying its claim.

Of course it's possible the gold wasn't in the specie room. There was the matter of the empty second-class cabin. When White Star's *Laurentic* went down in 1917 off the coast of Northern

---

[95] Riesenberg, Felix. *Standard Seamanship for the Merchant Service*, NY, NY: Nostrand Company, 1922, pps. 383-384.

Ireland, victim to a German mine, she went down with 3,211 gold bars in her second-class baggage room. Not as low as the orlop deck, the second-class baggage room of *Republic* was nevertheless on a lower deck. Maybe under water, maybe not. But difficult to access either way.

Regardless of accessibility, and regardless of what kind of chore it would have been to carry and transport heavy crates from one ship to another, it must be remembered that Sealby's belief at the time was that *Republic* would stay afloat. Why risk saving – and publicizing – a gold cargo that could more easily be off-loaded once *Republic* was safely towed in? Most likely, James Connolly's suspicions notwithstanding, any delay in employing *Baltic* to the task of taking aboard the passengers of *Florida* and *Republic* was due to caution. *Florida* wasn't sinking, after all, so the passengers were in no immediate danger. Given the fog, the number of ships in the vicinity, the relaying of communications between *Republic* and White Star officials in New York, the monitoring of changing weather conditions, it's not hard to imagine the prudent use of three or more hours to calculate the best, safest plan of action.

Not that rescuing the cargo and sending it over to *Baltic* wasn't at least discussed. Prudence dictates that it must have been at least considered as an option. Prudence and good business. According to salvage law, a salvor has rights even if his ship is of the same line. That means that *Baltic* would have had salvage rights. Or to put it another way, White Star would have had legal salvage rights for cargo lost on a White Star ship because the cargo would have been saved by another White Star ship. As such, according to law (and stipulated in the White Star bill of lading), White Star could have collected from those who shipped cargo aboard *Republic* to, at least, offset the salvage expenses. It might be recalled, however, that according to *Baltic*'s captain J.B. Ranson himself, echoing Sealby's opinion, *Republic* seemed in no danger of sinking. This obviates one of the three conditions for salvage rights, the one that says the ship must be in imminent peril. Besides, had *Baltic* saved *Republic*'s cargo, she would have had to have filed a salvage claim to collect. No evidence exists for such a claim. *Republic*, it seems certain, took her gold with her.

That *Republic* was resting on the bottom of the cold Atlantic didn't stop the immediate talk of possible salvage. But with the lack of technology available, the idea was, for the most part, quickly dismissed. Captain Alfred Sorenson, "one of the best-known wreckers on the coast," according the *New York Evening Sun* on January 25, 1909, "was asked what were the chances of raising the *Republic*. He said, 'they will never raise the *Republic*. She is reported to lie in 38 fathoms. You mark my words, she is a total loss. They won't even be able to get any cargo out of her.'" Captain W. Tal Dodge of the steamer *George W. Danielson* agreed in the *Providence Journal* the next day: "It will be impossible for a diver to work upon the sunken *Republic*, either in an attempt to bring the vessel to the surface or to recover sunken valuables." She was, simply, too deep. "It would mean certain death," Captain Dodge told the *Journal,* "to divers who ventured to go to the hold of the *Republic.*" Because of the extreme pressure at that depth, a diver would be "crushed like an egg shell," Dodge added. The *New York American* similarly reported that the general consensus among wreckers and other experts was that *Republic,* beneath 200 feet of water, "can only be considered a total loss."[96]

But not everyone was willing to so easily reject the idea of post-sinking salvage. The Arbuckle Wrecking Company conferred with White Star, presenting their idea of using huge magnets from a steamship, along with compressed air, to lift *Republic* off the ocean floor. If she was too deep for divers to safely get to her, then Arbuckle would simply go get her. According to the January 26th, 1909 *Christian Science Monitor,* officers of the Arbuckle company stated that there was a good possibility "of saving part of the cargo, consisting of imperishable goods." (Interesting word choice, imperishable.) Alas, the idea was only so much hopeful talk. Arbuckle's concept, at the time more science fiction than science, would come to nothing.

The difficulties given the depth weren't the only problems. To dive *Republic,* you first needed to find her. That was easier said than done. For one thing, there was no consensus on precisely

---

[96] *New York American,* January 26th, 1909, p.4.

where she went down. *Seneca* put her at latitude 40°25′30″, north, longitude 69°40′, west. *Gresham*, on the other hand, put her at 40°28′ north, 69°52′ west. The difference was eight nautical miles, which, in so far as finding her, might as well have been 800 given the technology of the time. Sonar was years away. Wrecks were found by running a cable between two ships and dragging it along the bottom, hoping to snag it on the lost ship. And that assumed you were in the right spot to begin with. In 1909, navigators didn't plug latitudes and longitudes into their GPS receivers to acquire satellite readings. They relied on celestial navigation and sextant readings and charts and dead reckoning. The famous case of the *Egypt* illustrates the difficulty. *Egypt* went down in 1922 carrying approximately $5 million in gold and silver. The search for her started almost immediately but it would take until August of 1930 before she would be found. The eventual recovery of the *Egypt's* treasure was considered an easier job than actually finding her.

To add to the confusion with *Republic*, the British Hydrographic Office Bulletin of 1909, distributed to the public at large and generally considered to be the last word on navigational matters, provided yet a third location, putting *Republic* at 40°28′40″ north, 69°38′40″ west. This turned out to be ten nautical miles distant from where she would eventually be found. Using the British Hydrographic Office location, and early 20th century technology, it would have been virtually impossible for anyone to have found *Republic*, let alone salvage her.

As for actually making a dive down to *Republic*, the problem was twofold. First, the depth. The risk of "being crushed like an egg shell," to borrow the words of Captain Dodge. As divers descend, they are exposed increasingly to greater pressures. The deeper the dive, the more water above the diver, the greater the pressure of the surrounding environment. In order to breathe normally, divers breathe gas equal to the surrounding pressure. As a diver's depth increases, his breathing gas dissolves into his body in much the same way that gas is dissolved into soda-pop. The longer the diver remains at depth, the more gas dissolves into his body. In order to allow this gas to come out of solution without forming dangerous (perhaps lethal) bubbles, the diver must gradually reduce the surrounding pressure, or "decompress," making pre-determined stops as he ascends, thereby reducing the pressure on his body gradually.

The second problem was one that was only starting to become recognized at the time and that was the problem of breathing compressed air. Oxygen toxicity from breathing high concentrations of compressed gases at elevated pressures can cause serious cell damage. Problems can include nitrogen narcosis, resulting in something akin to alcohol inebriation. More seriously, oxygen toxicity can result in seizures, even death.

In 1909, the dangers of depth and breathing weren't very well understood. The very first dive manual was published just four years earlier. Men like Scottish physiologist John Scott

Haldane were only beginning to make discoveries about the dangers of decompression, often by experimenting on themselves. Haldane invented a staged decompression procedure, a model arrived at more or less by trial and error. But it wouldn't be perfected for decades. In fact, it wouldn't be until the late 1950s/early '60s, as a result of offshore oil exploration, that a better understanding would come about of just how the human body reacts to the pressures of the deep. The fact is with 1909 technology, at over 40 fathoms where *Republic* lies (260 feet to be more precise), just 15 minutes of bottom time would require as much as several hours of decompression before a diver could safely surface. And a diver could make only one such dive a day.

Not that it might not have been tried. According to an article written by Teddy Remick in *Lost Treasure Magazine*, a salvage crew from England reportedly found *Republic* twenty years after she sank, and salvage operations commenced. [97] And then, just as quickly, ended. Though Remick's account cannot be confirmed, the supposed attempt "was a monumental task. Once through her hull, [the divers] found the companionway cluttered with a tangle of steel girders and plates blocking their path. The depth the divers had to work in, the unpredictable weather, and the huge sharks infesting the water eventually forced the salvage crew to give up and return to England." Recall the tons of Navy

---

[97] January, 1976, p.39.

food provisions aboard: the barrels of ham and sides of beef that would have attracted hosts of hungry sharks for decades to come. For many years, the best protector of the secret may have been the sea itself.

That was 1929. And so *Republic* would rest, untouched for 57 years, awaiting the technology that would one day make her and her cargo accessible. That technology would be the development of "saturation" diving, a technique that allows lengthy dives with a reduced risk of decompression sickness. It was discovered that if a diver remains at a certain depth over time, at some point, about 12 hours, an equilibrium is reached where the gas entering into the diver's blood and tissues is equal to the gas coming out of solution. At that point, the diver is "at saturation." Once saturation is reached, the amount of required decompression is maximized. In other words, once the diver reaches saturation, he requires only one (albeit lengthy) decompression procedure, regardless of any additional time he spends at depth. That means that once divers reach saturation, they can work an unlimited amount of time at depth without requiring any additional decompression. Decompression time for a diver who has been underwater for one day may be the same as for a diver who has been down for several weeks.

But once at saturation, the decompression procedure can last several days before the diver can safely "surface." And so saturation divers working from a salvage vessel live in a very controlled habitat on that vessel – a chamber kept at a pressure sufficient for the working depth. Divers transfer from their topside pressurized chamber through a pressurized transfer tube, to a pressurized diving bell, all the while remaining at their "working depth." When their target is reached (a shipwreck, for instance), they exit the diving bell and start their work. When they finish, perhaps hours later, the divers return to the diving bell which is then raised from the bottom and mated to the transfer tube. The divers come aboard into their pressurized chamber and live there at the near equivalent pressure of the working site's depth until their work is completed. When the job is done, they are then decompressed aboard their ship over the course of several days, at which time they can then safely leave the chamber.

With the development of saturation diving technology, it only remained for someone to come along and dive *Republic*. The technology isn't cheap, however. That someone needed to know there'd be a payoff. That someone needed to know about the treasure of *Republic*, the Tsar's secret – over $3 million in gold coins. Three-million, that is to say, in 1909 dollars. Potentially over a billion dollars today.

CHAPTER TEN

1987

"Red flag diver, swim to me,
Red flag diver, swim to me,
You'll be miserable, but I'll be free…"

— Aimee Mann, "Red Flag Diver"

In late 1983, I had been awarded salvage rights to *Republic*, having found her in '81 and having positively identified her in '83. Having cleared burdensome legal hurdles and unwarranted challenges, she was finally mine to salvage.

I had done some research, but I knew I needed to do more. I needed to learn everything I could about the ship and about her cargo. A successful expedition would be expensive. I needed to attract investors and that meant I needed to prove the existence of the rumored gold. Or I needed to prove the gold didn't exist. For as long as the possibility presented itself, I was captive to it. The matter was larger than mere curiosity and even larger than the possibility of great wealth. It was the Siren's song and I could not resist it.

By then I was married. Susan was a beautiful blonde, former Miss West Virginia runner-up whom I had met in 1981 while she was vacationing on Martha's Vineyard. We had hit it off right away. We dated and she moved to the Vineyard and we married in '82. She was intrigued by the search. She understood, I had thought. I had hoped, anyway.

The existence of the gold, as it turned out, wasn't easy to prove. Ironically, that's what made me certain I was on the right track. At first it wasn't the information I was finding that led me to believe the gold was aboard; it was the information that I wasn't finding. Virtually every important piece of information on *Republic* was missing or at least, ultimately, extremely difficult to come by. Serious efforts, it seemed to me, had been undertaken to make *Republic*'s secrets stay secret.

The first, most obviously missing piece was her very location. Why were there three sets of coordinates given as to where she sank, *none* of which were accurate? Why was the "official" location ten miles off? How could the United States government not have found her – resting in a busy shipping lane, no less – since she'd gone down, a period of time that included two world wars in which the navy routinely searched for enemy submarines and plotted sunken wrecks? She simply had to have been found. But *Republic* was glaringly conspicuous by her absence from the official charts.

The second thing that stood out was the lack of information about her construction. The plans I had wanted so that we could explore her nooks and crannies and all the potential places she might be hiding her treasure were non-existent. The schematics we had of the first and second and third class passenger areas were of little help, other than in informing us of where the gold most surely was not. What we needed were the details of the operational areas of the ship, the areas that were off-limits to passengers. We inquired of Harland and Wolff in Belfast but were told the plans had been destroyed by the German Luftwaffe in World War II. Plausible. Harland and Wolff, builders of aircraft carriers for the British Navy did, in fact, suffer at least two bombing raids in 1941. But further research revealed that the offices most likely containing the company's archived plans had remained untouched. This explains the existence of the plans of *Titanic*. In fact, one can find plans for the three ships that immediately preceded the construction of *Republic*: Harland and Wolff hull numbers 300 (the S.S. *Canada*), 315 (the S.S. *New England*), and 330 (the S.S. *Commonwealth*, which would ultimately become White Star Line's *Canopic*). The plans for hull number 345 (the next in the series), *Columbus* rechristened *Republic*, are nowhere to be found.

The ship's manifest for that January 1909 voyage across the Atlantic is conveniently missing as well. This document would, of course, reveal the cargo. It's simply gone. And yet with only a small amount of research, and maybe a little luck, you can find the manifest, as well as the construction plans, for any given 18th century Spanish galleon. But a certain ship from the early 20th century? Someone, somewhere, had done a masterful sanitizing job.

In '83 and again in '85, we undertook surveys of *Republic*. Using sonar we were able to get a clear picture of exactly how she was resting. And by then I had done more research, uncovering a good bit of the information that would confirm in my mind that *Republic* held a considerable gold cargo. I still didn't have the plans, though, and in 1985, I made a desperate attempt to find them by running advertisements in the Belfast newspapers, offering a £25,000 reward (roughly $50,000) for the plans of *Republic*. Maybe somebody, somewhere – a grandson or granddaughter, perhaps, of a Harland and Wolff employee from the early 1900s –, had the plans stuck away in a box in an attic or in a drawer in a cellar.

Coming up with nothing, I decided in 1986 that rather than continue to try to find plans that had obviously been made to disappear, I'd simply recreate them. For that, I hired Bob Stevens, a skilled naval architect who used to work for General Dynamics. In a *New York Times* article in 1987 (January 15th), Bob explained what we were up against. The sinking, Bob told the *Times*, was "like taking a 60-story building, shaking it violently and throwing it on its side." The task before us was finding the gold as Bob put it, "in an area the size of a broom closet." Bob, using his extensive knowledge and experience, set about reconstructing the plans of *Republic*.

I ended up having another legal challenge thrown at me in 1986. A nebulous salvage firm calling itself the Marshallton Group came along from New York, arguing in district court, in front of Walter J. Skinner – the very judge who had granted me salvage rights in '83 – that we hadn't been diligent in our efforts to salvage *Republic*. Three years had come and gone; they could do the job in 30 days, they claimed. I explained the processes we were going through, doing surveys of the ship, seeking structural plans, doing research, raising money. But Skinner sided – temporarily, anyway – with Marshallton. It didn't bother him that Marshallton was working with International Underwater Contractors, Inc., a company I had had talks with under a confidentiality agreement. But Skinner at least held Marshallton to their literal word; he gave them exactly 30 days to dive *Republic*. They dove. And I hired a U.S. marshal at the cost of $19,000 to accompany them on their boat. My plan was to place a claim on anything they brought to the surface; at least a finder's fee was owed, it seemed to me, since I was the one who discovered *Republic*'s resting place. But it was unnecessary. The end result of their work was nothing more than the ripping up of the ship's main deckhouse, ruining a formerly pristine wreck. Had they done their research, they would have known that the gold cargo would have been deep within the holds of the ship. They managed to bring up some silverware and plates and that was about it. Skinner gave the rights back to me.

With the discoveries from my research on the gold and with Bob Stevens reconstructing the ship's plan, I went in search of investors. I didn't have to look very far. As it happened, Bob had a brother-in-law with some money and a latent sense of adventure. Bob Polackwich was an oncologist in Tampa. He made a good living, but dealing with cancer patients every day can work on a guy's psyche. Certainly there were success stories, but there were also a lot of patients Bob got to know whom he ultimately couldn't help. And so when he got wind of *Republic* through Stevens, it seemed to him like just the kind of life-affirming project he needed. I flew down to meet with him in his sizeable home in the exclusive Avila neighborhood of Tampa and I went over what we'd found. He became more and more intrigued as I went over the evidence. We talked about the rumors; we talked about the possibility of there being earthquake relief aid aboard *Republic* and about the Navy payroll.

Then we talked about the Tsar's gold. I laid out the best argument I had at the time. I had done an extensive import/export analysis of gold on the New York exchange leading to the time of *Republic*'s departure. And a similar analysis for the Paris exchange. The discrepancy could explain the existence of a $3 million loss. Moreover, $3.5 million was supposedly aboard the White Star liner *Oceanic* which departed from New York on January 13th, 1909, just nine days prior to the *Republic* departure. The thing is, I couldn't find any proof that a $3.5 million cargo from *Oceanic* was ever delivered to Paris. Based on the rumors, the logical deduction was that the $3 million-plus was instead on *Republic*. It was at least enough to go on. Years later I would find out I was right about the $3 million, but for the wrong reasons. I identified the $3 million that I'd originally assumed was not on the *Oceanic* (and therefore aboard *Republic*) when I came across confirmation of that transaction within the Bank of France's internal documents. I confirmed that the original $3.5 million transaction was, indeed, aboard *Oceanic* and had been delivered safely. That particular transaction, at least, was not aboard *Republic*.

But I couldn't get past the idea of the rumors. And not just the rumors, but all the concealment. There had to be *another* shipment of gold. Another $3 million. I knew that the Russians were the most likely recipients. At first glance, however, I couldn't determine the need. After all, they had just closed a $250 million loan from the French, coincidentally on January 22, 1909, the very day of *Republic*'s departure. Russia certainly wouldn't need gold from New York, with all that money in Europe. But then I started looking deeper into all those newspaper reports about a "mysterious" short-term loan. A thirty-day loan at an unusually low interest rate. And then I looked closer at the actual $250 million loan documents found within several of the participating French bank's archives. The loan closed on January 22nd, but the first installment to Russia wasn't scheduled for disbursement by the

French banks for another 30 days, February 22. Exactly 30 days. The same length of time as the short-term New York loan that all the papers were reporting. Could the Russian financial situation have been that precarious? If it was, that would certainly explain the concealment. Like I said before: there's research, and then there's pit bull research. It all came together.

Right reasoning or wrong reasoning, the conclusion I'd come to in '86 was sufficient for Dr. Bob Polackwich. He roped in some doctor friends and we drew up a limited partnership, Sub Ocean Salvors International – SOSI. The biggest investment would be for our salvage ship. The *Oil Endeavor* was an out-of-service oil exploration ship that Polackwich actually found, 285 feet in length and equipped with a 40-ton crane and a saturation diving system good for a thousand feet. We rechristened her *SOSI Inspector*. Polackwich's idea. He was a big fan of Inspector Clouseau and the "Pink Panther" movies. I figured why not? Maybe she'd be clumsy like Clouseau, but Clouseau always seemed to crack the case in the end. All we needed was a crew. For that, we ended up acquiring Wolf Sub-Ocean Ltd., a major Canadian underwater contractor that was in bankruptcy. Between what *SOSI Inspector* came with and what we picked up from Wolf, we soon had everything we needed, including the proper staffing, three one-man Mantis Duplus submarines, three four-man deck decompression chambers, and a Scorpion remotely operated vehicle.

Our efforts soon started to attract the imagination of the

public. I was invited to appear on the *CBS Morning News* where I was interviewed by Diane Sawyer and on *Good Morning America* where I was interviewed by Kathleen Sullivan. *The New York Times* was doing stories on us and articles about our expedition were appearing in newspapers and magazines across the country, and around the world. It was getting exciting.

Finally, in July of 1987, we dove. We had a nine-man saturation diving team and a three-man bell team. Diving shifts would be 10 hours each with three men out-the-bell, 24 hours a day, seven days per week. But we ran into a big snag almost right away. I hadn't been paying close enough attention to Bob Stevens' efforts in reconstructing the plans of *Republic*. When he rolled them out, my heart sank. He hadn't done much more than redraw the original schematics of the passenger areas that I had made available to him. What he'd put together was wholly insufficient. Maybe he'd done his best with the information we had, I don't know. But there we were, four-point moored over *Republic* with divers already in the water. Every day was costing tens of thousands of dollars. I knew I needed to do something and I needed to act fast.

After we began the excavation based on our limited information, I took a launch back in and hopped on the next plane to London. We needed the Harland and Wolff plans; there was just no getting around it. I tried to track down descendants of Harland and Wolff employees from the early 1900s as well as descendants of *Republic*'s crew. I did an interview on London's ITV morning show and another on BBC radio. I offered the £25,000 reward again. But I came away empty-handed and it was back to the *SOSI Inspector*.

We decided to zero in on a certain target area of the ship that we felt would have lent itself well to the stowing away of a valuable cargo. Trying to find this target area – the broom closet of a 60-story collapsed building, as Stevens put it – wasn't easy. But we found it. The problem was that it was the wrong target. What we found was the ship's wine locker. There were thousands of bottles on board and we brought a few up and opened them in celebration of at least finding something.

For 74 days we explored *Republic*, digging through tons of debris and looking the entire time in all the wrong places. I'd find out later how close we'd come to where we now know the gold to be. But a few feet might as well have been a mile. All told, the 1987 expedition netted us hundreds of artifacts, including dinnerware, silverware, silver tea sets, bowler hats, crystal, the ship's anchors, and some damn fine bottles of nicely aged wine (one of them even made the cover of the October 31st issue of *The Wine Spectator*). But the Tsar's treasure, as well as Sperry's missing navy payroll, remained aboard.

The failure of that expedition would haunt me for years.

CHAPTER ELEVEN

Wreckage

"The cannons don't thunder, there's nothin' to plunder,
I'm an over forty victim of fate…"

— Jimmy Buffet, "A Pirate Looks at Forty"

There were some hard feelings after the 1987 expedition. A lot of people had lost a lot of money in the failed attempt. I didn't get paid myself, even though according to my agreement with SOSI, I'd been due a quarter of a million dollars in compensation, irrespective of results.

But shortly afterwards I managed to come across the plans of *Canopic*, the ship Harland and Wolff had built right before *Republic*. The two ships were remarkably similar and I hoped *Canopic*'s plans might be enough to allow us to find the exact location where we figured the gold would be. I approached Bob Polackwich with the idea of trying again in '88. He seemed interested, even though by then we were both questioning the conclusions I'd come to from the import/export analysis of New York gold – essentially the wrong $3 million that I'd focused on.

My wife Susan, meanwhile, had to move back to West Virginia where her parents still lived. By then, we'd lost our house and I was broke. I'd put everything we had into the '87 expedition. Ours was Susan's second marriage. Her divorce had resulted in a settlement for her of just about $19,000, the same $19,000 I had paid a U.S. marshal to protect our interests back in '86. And if she wasn't fond of me spending that money, she was even less fond of me pissing through all the rest of our money for what had become in her mind an ill-advised treasure hunt. We had two children by then but the marriage, as one might imagine, was reflecting a lot of the gloom from the failed expedition.

Initially she moved back to West Virginia with the kids while I stayed on Martha's Vineyard, still intrigued by *Republic* and hopeful that *Canopic*'s plans could help us strike literal gold. With no money I lived in my basement office, showering at a local health club, trying to make a few bucks as a real estate broker. But soon I followed Susan and the kids to West Virginia. I needed to save my marriage.

My experience protecting my legal rights to *Republic* had given me an education a lot of lawyers would envy and I determined that the best way to pick up the financial pieces would be to take advantage of that education. I finished two undergraduate degrees at Fairmont State College and then applied to the College of Law at West Virginia University. They were intrigued by the international media coverage I had garnered with *Republic* and I think they accepted me as much on the basis of diversifying the student body as on merit.

But *Republic* was still in the back of my mind. Maybe somehow I could continue with the research, prove the gold and convince Bob Polackwich and his investors that another trip would be worth every penny. But then, on April 23, 1988 – my birthday, as it happens – I received a phone call from Bob's attorney. Bob had been sailing a rented catamaran on the Intracoastal Waterway near Boca Raton, Florida. His nineteen-year-old son Jonathan had been with him. As the attorney explained, they were sailing between two small islands when somehow they lost control of the boat and it began to drift backwards, the mast coming into contact with a low-strung electrical power line. Both Bob and his son were electrocuted. It was a tragic and senseless freak accident. I had come to respect Bob. I appreciated his interest in our adventure, his hunger for wanting to pursue something exhilarating and life-affirming. Now Bob was gone. So, too, was any chance of making another dive to *Republic* in the foreseeable future. Our resources were gone. *SOSI Inspector*, our home for 74 days, would eventually be sold at auction. There would be nothing left.

I determined then that I was going to forget *Republic* once and for all, forget rumors about gold treasure. I would graduate from law school, pass the bar, hang my shingle in a nice quiet office building somewhere and make a decent living while raising my son and daughter and growing comfortably old with my beautiful wife. I was moving on.

But the marriage began to disintegrate further. Because I was broke, we had moved in with Susan's parents in their small farmhouse. Moving in with the in-laws is never a good thing. In time we separated, which is to say that I was kicked out. The best I could do was to arrange to see the kids as often as possible.

Now, divorced and virtually penniless, I withdrew from law school (although later was able to finish my MBA at WVU). But on top of the wreckage of *Republic* were now my marriage, my family, and my plans for becoming a lawyer. Legal troubles followed, the details of which exceed the bounds of this book, as well, no doubt, of the interest of the reader; a story for another time, perhaps. Suffice it to say that with the failed 1987 expedition, I came to wish I had never heard of *Republic*. I had succumbed to the Siren's call and true to form it had lured me to my destruction; the Siren's song had broken me.

Ultimately, destitute and surviving on food stamps, it was back to New York where I lived for quite some time with my mother, sleeping on her couch.

CHAPTER TWELVE

Calling Me

"So it seems dead men do tell tales, don't they?"

— Davy Jones, "Pirates of the Caribbean"

That damn ship.

Even before I moved to my mother's in New York, *Republic* was trying to lure me back. In 1998, while I was still in West Virginia, my mother called from her apartment in Manhattan. She'd been served with a subpoena. It was meant for me but apparently I'd been too hard to track down so it was delivered to her instead. Essentially it was legal notice that my rights to *Republic* were once again being contested.

William Cleary, a personal injury lawyer from Hackensack, New Jersey, had made a dive to *Republic* from a charter captain's boat. He'd brought up a porthole and some shards of pottery and decided to make a salvage attempt. He did a little research on

Republic and found out about the potential treasure, and about me, in pretty short order. By then I had posted a website about the ship and the potential gold cargo and if you searched for RMS *Republic*, my site came up first. (It still does.) The site was (and is) a comprehensive history of the ship and a *near*-thorough analysis (I still kept some of my cards close to the vest) laying out my argument, such as it was at the time, for the Tsar's treasure. My purpose was twofold. First, I wanted the website to serve notice that I was still actively pursuing the salvage, although admittedly by then my heart was far from in it. Research, too, is part of the salvage process and the research I'd done – the discovery, at least on paper, of the treasure, posted and clearly belonging to me – would warrant a share of the gold should anyone take it upon themselves to go get it. Second, I wanted the research to provide a challenge of sorts to anyone who wanted to take the time to attempt the refutation of my conclusions. If somebody wanted to find a hole in my reasoning and prove there was no gold aboard *Republic*, that'd be just fine with me. I'd lost enough to her.

Cleary found the website and became intrigued. I got wind of his plans even before the subpoena and at first I was happy to let him proceed with any salvage attempt he wanted to make. If he wanted to sink millions into the project, good for him. At best, if he found a billion dollars or so, I was at least owed a finder's fee since it was I who found *Republic* in the first place. Ten percent? Fifteen? Of a billion dollars, not a bad day's pay. At worst, if the gold wasn't there, well, he was more than welcome to all the port-holes and pottery shards he could find.

But when the subpoena subsequently arrived, I realized Cleary was trying to take me out completely. His argument was that I hadn't worked the site for over a decade and therefore had effectively abandoned the wreck. And he would further try to make the point that I hadn't earned even a finder's fee. I hadn't found *Republic,* so his argument went; *Republic* was clearly marked on the British Hydrographic Office chart some 70 years before I'd come along.

I knew I had to protect my rights. And so I left for New York. *Republic* had pulled me back.

What was in my favor was what I knew that Cleary ob-viously didn't know: the actual location. It wasn't, of course, where the official chart said it was. It wasn't even close. It was ten miles away, as a matter of fact. I smiled when I saw the coordi-nates Cleary was using. I knew what had happened. Locations of wrecks are the charter captain's stock in trade. If you're a diving hobbyist like Cleary, you need a charter captain to take you to the wrecks. But the captain's not going to just freely give you his in-formation. You can just rent your own boat if you know where the wrecks are. And so Cleary dove *Republic* without having any idea where – precisely – he was. He could have asked the captain, who apparently knew my coordinates, but the captain wouldn't have told him. So Cleary came ashore and promptly conferred with the official charts and assumed he then knew where *Republic* was resting. In reality, he didn't have a clue.

Inaccurate location notwithstanding, Cleary was still trying to work me out of the picture and I knew I needed some serious legal help. Into the picture came Tim Barrow, an admiralty and maritime law expert in Manhattan. The attorney I had at the time knew he was – no pun intended – in too deep. So he found Tim for me. Tim heard my story second-hand from my attorney and immediately assumed someone was pulling his leg. His client was a treasure hunter? Trying to maintain his claim to a *billion-dollar* treasure from a sunken White Star liner? It seemed fantastical. And then there was one other little thing. His client didn't have any money. Tim said something about getting back to my attorney and then hung up the phone. He was skeptical, but he was intrigued. Just weeks before he'd traveled to Greenwich, England, to Britain's National Maritime Museum to see the 75th anniversary *Titanic* exhibition. In his reception area was a lithograph of *Titanic*. Maritime law was a labor of love for him. That night he stopped off at the library, went online, found my website, and quickly discovered that I was for real.

Tim and I talked the next day and he told me we'd worry about his legal fees later. We needed to move fast to make certain Cleary stayed away from *Republic*. In time, Tim and I would come to an agreement – his valuable legal help for a piece of the action. It was all I had to offer.

Cleary tried to confirm his point that I hadn't produced any activity on *Republic* by noting that my original salvage action from 1983 had been dismissed "with prejudice". Tim flew to Boston and found that that was not the case. The action had simply been deactivated for lack of activity. There's a big difference. It wasn't as if my rights had been proactively dismissed by court order; there had simply been a lapse of time. So we took a two-pronged approach. We reopened the case in Boston, once again in front of Judge Walter Skinner, while defending my case in Newark, New Jersey against Cleary.

Skinner reopened the case but he set some conditions. We could proceed but we needed to notify anyone who might have a claim to *Republic*, to give them a chance to come forward. We agreed, but then did a quick dive of *Republic*, brought up a few artifacts as proof, and filed a brand new claim. We wanted our filing to be opened unconditionally. And when Skinner saw how serious we were, he agreed to consolidate both the 1983 action with our new filing. Now there were no conditions. That didn't necessarily mean exclusivity, however. Skinner left the door open for anyone who might come along with a legitimate claim.

Back in Newark, meanwhile, in district court, Judge John Bissell denied Cleary's request for an injunction to keep me from diving *his* location (as if I would want to), deciding that our two recorded locations were far enough from each other to present no conflict. Finally, on September 10th, 2001 (the day before 9/11, as it happened), Cleary's action was dismissed in Newark. He was free to try again in Boston, but he didn't get anywhere there either. The bottom line was that he could have anything he wanted from his erroneous coordinates; he just couldn't call his site *"Republic."* I read years later that Cleary begrudgingly gave me credit for my perseverance. "If in fact there's gold on the wreck," he told the *New Jersey Law Journal* in July of 2005, "and through the efforts of 20 years (Bayerle) receives it, he deserves it."

We kept seeking exclusive salvage rights once and for all and in 2005, Tim and I brought the matter before Judge Nancy Gertner in U.S. district court in Boston. Judge Gertner had replaced Skinner who had by then passed away. Gertner thoughtfully listened to our arguments as well as to the history of our salvage attempts. And she heard us recount the list of interlopers we had had to deal with over the years, the latest being the U.S. government itself. The Admiralty Division of the U.S. Department of Justice tried to use my own research to declare that they had a claim to the Navy payroll. I was flattered by the nod towards the accuracy of my argument and decided to regard it as a kind of confession that the payroll really had been on board. It's the closest the government has ever come to admitting it. Still, flattered or not, I argued that if the United States government wanted to make a claim, it needed to bring its own argument to the table, not mine.

Judge Gertner agreed. At a hearing, the D.O.J. argued weakly that they were relying on Judge Skinner's previous ruling that denied us exclusive salvage rights. "But this matter is now before me," said Judge Gertner. "What else have you got?" The suits who'd arrived for the hearing from Washington, D.C. were taken aback. They hemmed and hawed and finally Judge Gertner adjourned the hearing, telling them they'd have until 5:00 p.m. that day to deliver her a better argument and that she'd be making a decision by 6:00.

Judge Gertner seemed fascinated by the whole project. I don't imagine a case quite like ours had ever hit her docket. It was a grand, swashbuckling adventure to her. "Modern day pirates," she was fond of calling us, meaning it as a compliment and even using the phrase to describe us in her ruling. And her ruling was what we'd been looking for all along. The night of the hearing, Judge Gertner granted us exclusive salvage rights and injunctive relief from all others – including the United States government (they never did present a decent argument of their own) – who would presume to lay a salvage claim upon *Republic.*

The ship was now officially all ours to salvage.

By then I was back on my feet. It had been a struggle but I was ultimately able to regroup while living at my mother's. Adversity makes a clever man, goes a Russian proverb. When I began taking stock of my situation, I came to realize that the one thing I had been able to perfect over the years, by necessity, was my ability to do research. I knew my way around government archives, libraries, universities, financial institutions, you name it.

Domestic or international. I founded an archival research company and began working for private investigators, lawyers, authors, journalists, anybody who needed intricate, involved research. And business was good.

The research on *Republic* continued, as well. And it was shortly after that that I discovered the damnable $3.5 million receipt from the Bank of France, proving that the money I had originally thought was on board *Republic* wasn't on her after all. It was on *Oceanic*. The challenge I had laid out on my website for someone to poke a hole in my theory had been poked. I'd done it myself. Maybe the Navy payroll was still down there, but a billion dollars or more of gold coins originally headed for Russia was certainly not. It was devastating. All of the work, all of the research, all of the time and effort spent on legal maneuvering to eventually get the exclusive salvage rights – it had all come to nothing. I had wasted years.

Now, surely, I was finished with *Republic*.

But there were still those pesky rumors and they continued to haunt me. How to explain them? I couldn't help myself. With Tim's encouragement, I re-examined all the evidence, digging even deeper than before. Tim, too, had a lot to lose, after all. "Look," he said, "your research on the Navy payroll is beyond reproach. It's worth it for that alone. But the larger question is, why was the payroll kept secret all these years? There's got to be something else down there, something that someone wanted to

165

keep secret." When I ultimately found the thirty-day mystery loan and put it all together, we knew the rumors of the Tsar's treasure were true.

Republic had a hold of me again.

But that's the way it's been with *Republic*. Since the beginning. Since I first learned of her. I could have taken the settlement from my anti-trust suit and gone to St. Eustatius, but *Republic* called out to me. Then I went and found her even before doing the research, research that eventually led me to believe (wrongly) that the gold was nothing more than rumor, research that, had I done it first, would have stopped me before I'd even started. Then, after finding her, Cuz Daugherty came along and essentially did a free site survey for me, identifying the wreck and forcing me to lay a claim. Then, when I didn't have sufficient resources, Bob Stevens mentioned his well-heeled brother-in-law who just happened to be looking for an adventure. And when we needed equipment and the right ship, the *Oil Endeavor* came along. And then, when all I wanted to do was forget her, *Republic* pulled me back by sending Cleary into the picture, forcing me to go to New York and Boston where I was subsequently awarded all her salvage rights. And when I'd *really* given up, along came the epiphanous 30-day mystery loan pointing towards the veracity of the rumors.

And then there was this: during my research I had traveled to Vineland, New Jersey, Captain Sealby's boyhood home and where he eventually returned. I had discovered that at one time

Sealby was the president of the Vineland Historical Society. His personal papers had to be there. And in fact, that's where I would ultimately find the letter to him from his girlfriend, "the Rubber Ball", who had inquired as to what the British Board of Trade had been doing with him while he had been in London for that month. When I checked into the Vineland Holiday Inn the desk clerk asked if I wanted a smoking or non-smoking room. "Non," I said, and he handed me the key to room 345. It was, of course, *Republic*'s Harland and Wolff hull number.

But that wasn't the strangest thing. The strangest thing was walking though a Vineland cemetery looking for Sealby's grave. I felt compelled to pay my respects. I combed the cemetery for a couple hours and I never found it. Dusk was falling and I decided to give up and I began walking towards my car, taking the shortest route through the cemetery, wanting to get out of there before it became dark. Within yards of my car, something – I don't know what – made me turn around and glance downwards and that's when I saw it, after two hours of single-mindedly looking for it: "Inman Sealby – 1862-1942." The moment gave me goose bumps and I stood there for some time, until the sun disappeared and the sky grew dark. Then I got in the car and drove back to room 345 of the Vineland Holiday Inn, more determined than ever.

Captain Sealby had a secret, you see. He knew. He knew what Roosevelt and Churchill knew and what White Star no doubt knew. But he had kept it to himself. The consummate company man, the loyal captain. But maybe some secrets aren't meant to stay secret forever, and maybe Captain Sealby was trying to get my attention that evening. Hell, maybe it hadn't even been *Republic* that had been calling me. Maybe it had been Sealby all along.

Chapter Thirteen

Gold Never Rusts

"The four most beautiful words in our common language:
'I told you so.' "

— Gore Vidal

Here's what Captain Inman Sealby knew, what he must have known: at least $3.8 million of gold was aboard his ship. $800,000 was bound for Gibraltar for the U.S. Navy; $3 million was bound for Gibraltar to be transferred to a Russian ship and subsequently delivered to Tsar Nicholas II.

Here's how we know about the Navy shipment. Every month, for the duration of the Great White Fleet's around-the-world cruise, approximately half a million dollars was delivered to Paymaster Samuel McGowan, save for one month: February, 1909. The record of that disbursement is missing. The fleet distributed $300,000 of its own provisions to Messina for earthquake relief. It would have needed replacing. By mid-January, Teddy Roosevelt, like a proud papa to his fleet, made certain, through an act of Congress, that $800,000 was made available to McGowan, which would cover the February disbursement, plus reimburse the fleet for the supplies sent to Messina. *Republic* was scheduled to rendezvous with the fleet on February 2nd. She never arrived. And on January 24th, the very day of her sinking, Rear Admiral Charles S. Sperry, commanding the Great White Fleet, strangely ordered the *Yankton* home ahead of the fleet with orders to pick up $800,000. Sperry, meanwhile, refused to allow his sailors to enjoy shore leave in Gibraltar, their last port of call before sailing home, an exercise, had it taken place, that would have required immediate payment to the sailors in gold.

And of course we know a lot more. The details are in Chapter Seven. The fact is, every piece of evidence found, along with evidence that is conveniently missing, points to the idea that $800,000 was expected in Gibraltar and $800,000 never arrived in Gibraltar. Between the expectation and the non-arrival of the funds was the sinking of the RMS *Republic* (and with her, it must be remembered, was the reported loss of U.S. Navy "provisions").

The secrecy over the missing $800,000 can be explained, perhaps, by Roosevelt's vanity ("Without a scratch…not an accident worthy of mention…") or, more likely, a desire to keep something even bigger a secret. A secret that, had it come to light in 1909, might well have created the conditions for a sea-change in the balance of European power. The potential fallout might have cost Russia her immediate financial stability. The Bolsheviks might have been encouraged to come to power eight years earlier than they did, splitting Russia off from her alliance with France and creating a golden opportunity for Germany that Kaiser Wilhelm II would have found impossible to resist. France would have fallen to Germany in short order, World War I would have ended practically before it began, and the history of the twentieth century would have been largely altered.

That secret was a $3 million short-term loan from a New York bank (the Guaranty Trust Company of New York?) or banks, shipped aboard *Republic*. We know this because, among other things, we know a $3 million, 30-day mystery loan at a below-market interest rate was announced on January 15th, 1909 and the only entity creditable enough to receive such a loan would have been a sovereign government, and a sovereign government that was in a position to pay the loan back. 1909 Tsarist Russia meets the criteria nicely. The Russians had motive (a desperate need, in fact), they had the means ($18 million coming to them in a month from French banks), and they had the opportunity – one Gregory Wilenkin, Russian financial agent, arriving in New York the day before the mystery loan was announced and departing the day after *Republic* left New York harbor.

And as with the Navy funds, we know a lot more. The details are in Chapter Eight. The fact is, every piece of evidence found, along with evidence that is conveniently (and conspicuous-ly) missing, points to the idea that $3 million was aboard *Republic* to save the Tsar.

We know on the ship where the money is not. The 1987 expedition focused mistakenly on the wine locker. Research since then has narrowed the possibilities to three potential locations. The first is the ship's specie room, located most likely at the very bottom of *Republic*. The second is the second-class storage area, cleared out prior to departure from New York with second-class passengers moved to first class. The third is the area on the ship where the provisions to replace *Culgoa*'s provisions were held. We've run the numbers and uncovered an 8,000-pound discrep-ancy between what the government claimed was aboard, and what was really aboard as calculated using the government's own figures (see Chapter Five). Even further research, available only to investors in our upcoming expedition, has narrowed the possibili-ties from these three locations to the one true location.

And now the proverbial bottom line. What is the worth of *Republic*'s cargo? On the surface, it seems that the easiest, quickest way to calculate it would be to take into account the factor of time. Put simply, what is $3.8 million from 1909 worth today? If we want to consider the effects of inflation, we could use the consum-er price index over the long period of years from 1909 to the pres-ent. This calculates today's *purchasing power* of 1909's $3.8 million.

Doing so yields us a current value of $96.9 million.

But we could also measure the effects of inflation by using *economic power*. We could consider the amount in question as a percentage of the economy of the United States (with economy defined as gross domestic product), and make a comparison based, essentially, on the amount of "influence" $3.8 million had in 1909. If we take the same percentage of GDP, the same amount of influence, we find that $3.8 million in 1909 is the equivalent today of $1.78 *billion*.

There are still other ways to measure worth based on time value, including labor value, income value, opportunity cost, etc.[98] These ways put our value somewhere between purchasing power and economic power. So, looking strictly at time value, it's probably sufficient to think of the $96.9 million as worst case and the $1.78 billion as best. But obviously that's quite a range. Is there a better way of determining value?

In the particular case of *Republic*, we mustn't forget the nature of the cargo with which we're dealing. Measuring relative worth as a function of time is all well and good for making comparisons between given years. But aboard *Republic*, we don't just have $3.8 million that needs to be adjusted for time. We have a commodity; namely: gold. A commodity that has a specific current market value. And if we know the amount of gold, we can then

---

[98] For an excellent discussion of relative worth, including an interactive calculator, I recommend a visit to www.measuringworth.com.

determine the overall value. How to determine the amount? Well, we know that the amount of gold, whatever it is, was worth $3.8 million in 1909. And in 1909, the price of a troy ounce (the standard of measure) of gold was $18.96. At the time of this writing, a troy ounce is worth $1,729.00, or roughly 91 times what it was worth in 1909. Three-million, eight-hundred thousand dollars in gold multiplied by 91 is $346 million. Let's call that our new worst case for the treasure.

But our new best case rightly takes into account more than just weight. We can assume fairly safely that the $3.8 million aboard *Republic* was in gold *coin*. The $800,000, most certainly. We know from the records that the Navy took its disbursements in gold and we know that the sailors would have been paid in coin. Gold bars, that is to say, would have been completely impractical. Each ship's paymaster would have made his requisition from the fleet paymaster (McGowan) in specific denominations of coinage, based on what he felt was the most practical and useful composition.

As for the Tsar's loan, we can assume U.S. gold coins, as opposed to anything else, including gold bars, for a variety of reasons. First, the loan would have been in U.S. dollars. Loans were in the currency of the realm, as exemplified by Japan's $22 million bond proceeds in 1905, received by the Bank of France entirely in coin. If you come to New York to borrow money, you're going to receive it in dollars. And the most practical way to ship dollars was in gold coin; namely, the $20 gold double eagle (so called because the ten-dollar gold coin was referred to as an eagle). The double eagle was the highest denomination available. Gold bars might have been preferred for investment and exchange, but a short-term emergency loan, which is essentially what the Tsar's loan was, would have required the liquidity that dollars, in the form of gold coin, would have allowed. As confirmation of the practice of loaning gold coins, the $3.5 million that I chased down that was ultimately aboard *Oceanic* was in $20 double eagles. And interestingly, the import/export analysis I had done while on the trail of *Oceanic*'s cargo indicated a shortage at that time of gold bars in New York. Coins were shipped as a matter of necessity. And let's not forget the rumors. They always specified gold coins and, in particular, double eagles.[99]

For our purposes, therefore, the most appropriate measure of *Republic*'s treasure would be its *numismatic* value. Our attention must therefore go to the collectible value of the $20 gold double eagle. And the collectible value of coins is, to a large degree, based on condition. What can we know about the condition of the coins aboard *Republic*? We can know this: loans in coinage were typically made with newly-minted coins. Over time, abrasion through normal wear affects the actual weight of a gold coin. For this

---

[99] U.S. paper money, in case you're wondering, would have been unacceptable overseas. A paper bill, essentially a promissory note drawn on a U.S. bank, would have had almost no practical value to someone in Russia or Europe. Gold, on the other hand, in bars or stamped out as coin, is obviously a valuable commodity in its own right.

reason, bankers preferred to deal in uncirculated, or nearly-uncirculated, gold coins. It's a safe assumption that the Tsar's $3 million loan was in $20 double eagles (150,000 of them) that were near mint condition, if not mint. We can also say this: gold doesn't rust, tarnish, or corrode. Even in saltwater. The safest place for uncirculated gold coins, to ensure zero wear and tear over time, might just be at the bottom of the ocean, out of the reach of human hands. If you were looking to make a long-term investment (long term over a century or more!), you could do a lot worse than taking $3 million of uncirculated gold coins, loading them aboard a ship that is destined to sink, and then coming back 100-plus years later to retrieve them.

The Navy shipment is another story. We can't say what the condition of the Navy coins might have been. Coins in an uncirculated condition were not at all necessary for the sailors. So for simplicity sake, let's assume the above inflation factor for gold of 91 for our Navy coins. That means a worth today of $72.8 million for those alone, which we will temporarily set aside.

Now let's consider the Tsar's coins. What's the value of an uncirculated, 1909, $20 gold double eagle? This is where things get interesting. The American Numismatic Association, the standard bearer for coin dealers and collectors, uses a grading system to designate condition. Mint-state coins (MS) range from 60 to 70, with 60 being an uncirculated coin that might have minor scratch marks or other slight flaws and a 70 coin being essentially perfect in its condition. The beautiful Saint-Gaudens double eagle (available starting in 1907 and therefore the most likely candidate to be aboard *Republic*), ranges in value, according to the well-respected "Red Book" guide to coin values, from around $2,000 to $8,000 for a specimen of MS63 condition, depending on how many were minted and where.[100] Scarcity, besides condition, is the other factor affecting value. But for a coin with a higher condition than MS63, one has to look at coins that have been sold at auction or are, perhaps, up for sale on eBay or by dealers who specialize in rare coins. For Saint-Gaudens double eagles from 1907-1909 that are in MS65 to MS70 condition, the numbers are staggering, averaging $20,000-$40,000 a piece or more. A single 1908-S, MS67 sold at auction in January of 2012 for $161,000. For all we know, there are 150,000 of those on board *Republic*. That's 24 billion dollars' worth.

Of course that's far too optimistic. And naturally the concept of scarcity gets a bit lost if suddenly the market is flooded with 150,000 of the same coins (our goal, naturally, would be to control the sale of the coins for this reason). But even if we assumed, say, $5,000 per coin, which does not seem at all unreasonable, we're looking at a total value of three-quarters of a billion dollars. Add the Navy cargo into the mix, and we get closer and closer to a billion.

What puts us over a billion (*way* over) is a little something

---

[100] Yeoman, R. S.,; *Guide Book of United States Coins, 2013: The Official Red Book* (Kindle Locations 5145-5146). Ingram Distribution. Kindle Edition.

called the concept of provenance. Would you rather have a 1908 Saint-Gaudens double eagle in MS-65 condition that you buy from a coin dealer, or a 1908 Saint-Gaudens double eagle in MS-65 condition that was part of a cargo bound for Tsar Nicholas II aboard a White Star liner that sunk after colliding with another passenger ship in heavy fog off the coast of Nantucket in 1909? *That's* the concept of provenance. It's why people pay $25 for a chunk of coal salvaged from *Titanic* that otherwise would be worth less than one-tenth of a penny. And if coal can fetch such a mark-up, how much more of a mark-up could a double eagle gold coin fetch? These are not coins; these are museum pieces.

My estimate, and I submit that it is a conservative one, is that the Tsar's treasure, the secret of the RMS *Republic*, coupled together with the missing Navy payroll, is worth somewhere in the neighborhood of *one and a half billion dollars.*

≈≈≈≈≈≈≈≈≈

In 2005, Tim Barrow and I secured full salvage rights to *Republic* in Judge Nancy Gertner's courtroom in Boston, Massachusetts. But in 2011, we were able to take things one very big step forward. Having eliminated every other claim (including the U.S. government's), and having no further challenges come forward, we were able to secure actual title to the ship.[101] Ownership. The White Star liner *Republic* now belongs to me. My ship has come in.

But damned if it isn't just a little inconveniently placed. Then again, if it were easy to get to, somebody may have absconded with the treasure by now. As it is, the treasure, all $1.5 billion of it, lies safe and secure, 40 fathoms under the sea, still as shiny as it was on the morning of January 22nd, 1909 when it was loaded aboard *Republic*. And of the analogous 60-story building shaken violently and thrown on its side, I know where the broom closet is.

The expedition we are currently putting together will run about $8 million per season. We're currently assembling our stakeholders. They know that, in the end, their investment will be a small price to pay for a treasure worth well over a billion dollars. And I feel compelled to say that it actually compares pretty favorably to the price one modern day pirate has paid. But the cost of most of my adult life chasing *Republic*'s treasure will be repaid not so much with gold coins as with peace of mind. How, after all,

---

[101] *See* Photos & Exhibits, Exhibit-AT.

can you put a price tag on one magnificent, hard-earned, richly deserved "I told you so"? The Tsar's century-old secret will be no longer secret. The proof will be in crates aboard our salvage ship. Stacks of twenty-dollar gold double eagles. And I'll be standing over them, admiring the fruits of what has been the pursuit of a lifetime, and one hell of a ride.

It'll be liberating... It'll be glorious.

The End

Addendum

The Legacy of *Republic*

In the White Star literature, a great deal was made about the luxury of the RMS *Republic*. Appropriately so. The dining saloon was "spacious and well-furnished" and "the wainscoting (was) in polished hard woods, light in colour, whilst the upholstery (was) of rich texture." The literature continued:

> The other public rooms of this fine steamer are proportionately capacious and comfortable. The Library calls for special mention; with its well stocked book-cases and luxurious chairs and settees, it is indeed a veritable "Temple of Rest" to those who seek a quiet nook to con the latest work of a favourite author. But, however tempting it may be, the old voyager will perhaps say he wishes for nothing more cosy than the Smoke Room; nor can the taste of such an one be impugned, as everything that experience can devise for the smoker's comfort is here apparent.
>
> A notable feature of the steamer is the Lounge, always in great request in wet weather. Situated on the promenade deck it is peculiarly the ladies' domain, giving place to no other apartment in the cheeriness of its aspect.

More than luxury, however, it becomes clear reading the literature what was really important to passengers in 1909: comfort and relaxation. Contrast White Star's descriptions of *Republic* with the descriptions of today's mega cruise ships, each with multiple restaurants (with world-class chefs) and nightclubs and coffee shops and planned activities and first-class entertainment (some boast Broadway shows) and attentive crews that number more than *Republic*'s full complement of passengers. Cruising today requires variety and entertainment, not just comfort. But in 1909, the "cruise" was not an end in and of itself (even if today's cruises do often sail to exotic locations). In 1909 the ships were called ocean liners. Nobody called them cruise ships. The destination was the thing. It was the way – the only way – you were able to go from the United States to Europe and back. They still have transatlantic cruises, of course, but even those are more about the journey than they are about arrival. In 1909, the choice to fly from New York to London in eight hours wasn't available.

And for passengers in 1909, comfort and relaxation meant, above all else, feeling safe. If the ships were appointed with heavy, upholstered chairs in their libraries, it was to make you feel as though you might be sitting in the lobby of a luxury hotel, not in a room that was moving at 16 knots over the unsteady waves of the ocean. The objective was to make you forget you were even on a ship.

But for White Star, in addition to comfort and security, speed became a factor as well, forced upon them by the demands of the marketplace. Cunard's ships were faster. For White Star it became acceptable to compromise safety for speed so long as the designs of the ships (all the way down to those heavy, upholstered chairs) presented the *appearance* of safety. But whether it was steaming through fog or a field of ice, speed would prove fatal. The hubris of the time, however, prevented thoughts of disaster. The "modern" steamships had watertight compartments and were "practically unsinkable."

Titanic was steaming at about 22.5 knots when she hit the iceberg that doomed her. By the time the iceberg was spotted looming out of the darkness ("Iceberg right ahead!"), *Titanic's* fate was sealed. It would all come out at the inquiry, of course. Along with another deadly circumstance born of hubris: the shortage of lifeboats. What need for lifeboats on a practically unsinkable ship?

It remains, then, to wonder at what might have come about from a public inquiry on the sinking of *Republic*. Perhaps the real legacy of *Republic* is the fact that she didn't enjoy the legacy she could have, the legacy she should have: a warning that, properly heeded, might have saved the lives of 1,517 people just three years later.

We don't know what speed Sealby was doing in the fog. We have unofficial statements from company officials (who were not under oath when they signed them) stating that the ship's speed was reduced during the fog and that the ship's whistle was sounded regularly. That may all be true. It may be true, as well, that the S.S. *Florida* proceeded likewise through the fog. But the fact remains that the two ships collided. Yes, it was a busy shipping lane, but the collision of two ships in heavy fog, even in a busy shipping lane, is hardly a foregone conclusion.

And one must remember that for this particular trip, speed was important for reasons outside of passenger expectations. *Republic* was required in Gibraltar. Roosevelt's fleet was waiting to rendezvous with her, ostensibly to receive barrels of ham and potatoes and onions and salt. But perhaps the sailors were also awaiting their pay. And perhaps a Russian ship or two was awaiting a little something for the Tsar.

An inquiry would have also shed light on the lifeboat situation. For hours upon hours, the lifeboats were rowed first between *Republic* and *Florida* and then *Florida* and *Baltic*, making multiple trips between each ship, taking full loads of passengers across and then coming back empty to load up again. The argument might have been made in a public inquiry in White Star's defense that the ability to now send a C.Q.D. distress call, coupled with the slow rate of descent for a modern ship equipped with watertight compartments, made a full complement of lifeboats unnecessary. *Republic* proved, did it not, that rescue ships could be summoned in short order and that modern ships could float for hours if not days?

Still, the general public would have been made aware that steamships, as a matter of course, had inadequate lifeboat capabilities. The reason for the inadequacy? Lifeboats cluttered the deck. They obstructed passenger views. They were inconvenient. And perhaps more important than anything, the British Board of Trade simply didn't require lifeboats in numbers sufficient to carry all the passengers and crew.

The lack of lifeboats was an evident concern to at least one observer. A letter to the editor of the *New York Herald* from passenger S. C. Halberstadt "On board the steamship *Baltic*, Jan. 23, 1909" and printed January 26th, addressed the situation with hard numbers. "This steamer, for example, has certificate to take…2,411 persons," the letter said, "but has only…accommodations for saving passengers and crew in case of wreck (sufficient for a) total of 1,372. Where are the remaining 1,039 to go in such a case?" Mr. Halberstadt's prescient letter ended ominously: "While everything came out all right, there could just as well have been a big loss of life…"

The *Titanic* disaster directly resulted in changes in maritime regulations, changes that, had they come about as a result of the *Republic* sinking instead, would have saved, perhaps, most if not all of the passengers and crew aboard *Titanic*. Requiring a sufficient number of lifeboats for all passengers and crew was the obvious regulation. But had it been shown that speed was a factor in *Republic*'s demise, *Titanic*'s lifeboats might not have been even necessary that night. The negative publicity White Star would have had to endure from a public revelation that *Republic* was steaming at 16 knots in near-zero visibility may have been enough to ensure a more deliberate path through the ice field for *Titanic*. Or perhaps a different path. Sealby himself was quoted on the matter of speed in *Titanic*'s case in the April 22nd, 1912 *New York Times*. "I would recommend that steamship commanders be ordered to take the southern track," he said with respect to the dangers of ice, but then added this as well: "and always travel slowly in fog, under penalty of dismissal." Was this an ironic dig at White Star? The opposite, in fact, may have been the case in 1909. Sealby's orders from White Star (and orders, after all, are always made under an unspoken threat of dismissal) might have been full speed ahead and not "travel slowly."[102]

Sealby had other things to say, as well, notably about the bulkhead construction, another factor in the demise of both ships, and yet another factor that would only come to light with the *Titanic* inquiry. "Watertight bulkheads should be constructed as strong as the hull itself," he said in that same *New York Times* interview. *Republic*, Sealby knew as well as anyone, was hit with the same kind of glancing blow as *Titanic* – along the length of the ship, cut under the waterline. Both ships were designed by the

---

[102] The White Star Lines Regulations set out mandatory guidelines that all captains were required to follow for safety reasons. As in the case with the *Egypt*, however, these regulations may come second in priority to commercial interests when shipping valuable cargo on a tight shipping schedule. See the reference to the *Egypt* in Chapter Two.

same design team and constructed by the same builder with the same steel from the same source using the same rivets.

Speed, lifeboats, construction – it would all have come out three years earlier than it did. With hearings, depositions, and sworn testimonies, the public would have heard in 1909 what it had to wait to hear in 1912 when it was much too late for over 1,500 souls.

Curiously, *Republic* wasn't allowed to present itself as much of a lesson in all that could go wrong even after *Titanic* sank. The man who could have spoken from experience most eloquently on the above issues was never officially asked to speak. Captain Inman Sealby, with 25 years of experience with White Star and commanding a White Star ship that sunk in very similar circumstances as *Titanic* – just three years prior! – was never put under oath during any of the *Titanic* proceedings.

What might Sealby have revealed? Surely questions of cargo would have come up. Sealby was a loyal company man, but by all accounts also an honest one. Under oath, he would most likely have answered all questions put to him truthfully. Interestingly, he seemed to want to do just that, hoping throughout his life that he would someday get the opportunity to testify as to what he knew about *Republic*. He left White Star in 1909 and began studying maritime law at the University of Michigan, eventually opening a practice in San Francisco. He returned to the sea just a few years later, serving as a transport captain with the U.S. Merchant Marine

during World War I. Later he served as a member of the United
States Shipping Board, retiring in 1930 and returning to Vineland.
But way back in 1911, while still in law school, he was quoted in
the April 19th *New York Times*, in an article about his law career
plans, as saying that he hoped one day, "if he lives to be a very
old man," as the *Times* put it, "to take part in the trial of the suit
over the collision between the *Republic* and the *Florida*." As a very
old man? Apparently even then he must have realized the secrecy
surrounding *Republic* wasn't going to go away any time soon.

But Inman Sealby died at the age of 80 without ever having a chance to say on the record whatever it was that he wanted
to say. What got in his way? Jack Binns, the heroic radio operator,
claimed it was legal maneuvering. In an article in the *Vineland
Historical Magazine* in 1943 (Vol. XXVIII, page 50), speaking on the
event of Sealby's death, Binns declared his admiration for a man
who was rendered "unable to clear himself, because of a web of
legal weaving (that) prevented the investigation that would give
him that opportunity."

We don't know what the "legal weaving" was. But we
can be certain that nothing less than something very significant
was attached to *Republic*, something important enough to squelch
forever a public investigation and hearing, something that forced
Inman Sealby to take a secret to his grave. The secrecy. Perhaps
that's the legacy of *Republic*. For who's to say that Roosevelt
and Churchill's apparent decision to bury any potential public

mention of the cargo was the wrong decision? Fifteen-hundred lives balanced against a Europe that might have looked decidedly different and more dangerous had the Tsar's financial situation been revealed. With a Germany that might have moved quicker. Much quicker. To be fair, Roosevelt and Churchill could not have anticipated the *Titanic* disaster.

Or could they have? What was Sealby able to tell them during the private inquiry? We may never know. All evidence points to the fact that such an inquiry was held, but no details of it seem to exist.

But the shroud of secrecy is lifting. Captain Inman Sealby may yet get his opportunity to speak, at least in a sense. And as the potential for being the richest sunken treasure discovery of all times, it could be that *Republic*'s true legacy awaits.

Acknowledgments

This book represents much more than just a book. It represents the culmination of more than 30 years of a life's work, work that, at times, was very tedious and unforgiving. There have been many, many people that have helped me along my quest, and if your name isn't among the few listed below, it is not that I have forgotten your contribution. And although I admit I do like to maintain a certain degree of control in my pursuits, I know that this journey was intended for many more than just one individual. It has spanned multiple generations, and there have been many, both friends and adversaries, that have passed on since its inception. My biggest wish is that I could have you all stand with me as we see this through to its completion, as we finally put the mystery of *Republic* to rest.

To start, I'd like to thank all the workers at the various records facilities I've worked in over the years. You have all been very gracious with your time and patience, for what I'm sure appeared as an eccentric and often exhausting hunt for obscure documents. This includes personnel in: the U.S. National

Archives and Records Administrations facilities in Washington D.C., College Park, Philadelphia, and New York; the Library of Congress; the U.K. National Archives (formerly the Public Record Office); the Archives Nationales Françaises; Harvard University; Princeton University; Columbia University's Rare Book and Manuscript Library; the Morgan Library; the Bibliothèque Nationale de France; the archivists of Crédit Lyonnais, Société Général, BNP Paribas, and Barings. Again, your help has been critical, and your patience worthy of praise. I'd also like to thank Klaus Normann Petersen, Isabel Hohneck, and Karim Annabi for your assistance with some of the European research.

My thanks, too, to those who have moved on to other projects. Special thanks to my first admiralty attorney, Dean Cycon. We had some great times.

Not all the assistance has been related to research, however. On a lonely, uphill quest the greatest assets have been the people that join along the way. I'd like to thank my friends and family for their continual support, through both storms and calm seas. Special thanks to my childhood friends Harry Demell, Paul Ogman, and Jack Dornberg, whose friendship over 50 years has offered nothing but understanding and encouragement (and many good memories). Thanks also to my Island friends, including Norman Gardner, Jim and Jeanne Crave, and Paul Adler, who have offered much encouragement since we became friends on the island so many years ago. Thanks also to my ex-wife, Susan, who hung in there as long as she could, despite the hardships. I know it wasn't easy to do.

I will always remember those who have been called to their final harbor, of the deceased "crew," my thoughts go to: Dr. Robert Polackwich whose quest for adventure propelled the first effort; and Gerard Spring, my publicist. Gerard, you did an excellent job. And I have some of my very fondest memories of my former in-law family who have since passed on, Granny, Poppi and my former brother-in-law, Beau, and Teetie – you all rooted me on! I wish you could all be here to see the denouement. I'd also like to thank my Uncle Warren Hartmann who said "Martin will do this!," and my father, Gerry, who started my life of adventure, introducing me to *Good Old Coney Island* and the brigantine *Vineyard*, and for his support through some rough times. I wish they all could still be around to see this through.

As to the living, of course, my great gratitude to my kind mother, Ruth, without her assistance for a number of years, and inspiration/motivation, I may very well be sleeping in a refrigerator box under a bridge somewhere.

Lastly, I'd like to thank those who have recently had a great effect on this book and the RMS *Republic* project as a whole. A thank you to Charlie Haas, Bob Evans, and Bob Cembrola for their suggestions and reviews of the *The Tsar's Treasure* manuscript. I'd like to thank Jerry Payne, my co-author, who's passion for history and love for the sea have been essential in conveying my research and story in an ideal fashion. My exceptional maritime lawyer, Tim Barrow, who was been elemental in keeping the project alive and achieving the great milestone of obtaining legal title to *Republic*. I'd like to thank my beautiful daughter, Tessa, for her continuous positive influence and support. I enjoy every second we spend together, and she never fails to bring a smile to the face of this old salt. And last but not least, to my son, Grant, whose involvement over the past few years has been critical in moving things forward. He both speaks loudly and carries a big stick in his management of this project. Without his persistence and diligence, this book would have likely never been written.

And to anyone that has ever followed or supported this project since its inception more than 30 years ago, I appreciate not only your interest in the project, but your belief in me. Again, thank you!

NOTES ON SOURCE MATERIAL

Throughout this book I have endeavored to footnote as best I could the source material that I have relied upon in my research. In the case of facts that are merely interesting in so far as the narrative is concerned, I have often noted the source (a contemporaneous newspaper account, for instance) within the body of the text. For notations that are more relevant with respect to the actual argument herein of lost treasure, I have footnoted with more detail (page/column numbers, etc.). I have also included especially interesting photos and evidentiary exhibits in the Photos & Exhibits section as well as the Appendix that follows. It must be remembered, however, that the sourced research within these pages represents a fraction of the research that I have undertaken. It simply is not possible to include it all here. Much of it is extremely detailed. Collectively, it is thorough and comprehensive. And it is, I think, persuasive, not so much adding to what has been presented here as corroborating it. Much is publicly available on our website: http://www.rms-republic.com. More is available to our investors. The reader is invited to visit us online for further information.

Nearly all photos, postcards, and newspaper clippings of *Republic*, her crew, and the collision I have used from my own private collection. Photos of the Great White Fleet at Gibraltar were from the Naval History and Heritage Command's Archives (http://history.navy.mil/index.html) or from the (sourced) collection listed at (http://www.greatwhitefleet.info/GWF_Gibraltar. html). The photo from the 1981 Expedition was offered courtesy of Kent Guernsey.

Appendix

I.

Reported U.S. Government Cargo Aboard *Republic*

Journal of Commerce	U.S. Claim Net Weight	Unit, Net	Gross Weight	Unit, Gross
816 Hind quarters beef	211141 lbs. Fresh Beef	162.17 lbs./quarter	122362 lbs.	149.95 lbs./quarter
486 Fore quarters beef	included in above	avg. fore and hind	91383 lbs.	188.03 lbs./quarter
280 carcasses sheep	13128 lbs. Fresh Mutton	46. 88 lbs. /carcass	13408 lbs.	47.89 lbs. /carcass
554 boxes pork loins	40890 lbs. Fresh Pork	73. 8 lbs. /box	47863 lbs.	86.39 lbs. /box
340 sides Veal	24814 lbs. Fresh Veal	72.98 lbs./side	25494 lbs.	74.98 lbs./side
600 cases frankfurters	15000 lbs. Frankfurters	25 lbs./case	18500 lbs.	30.83 lbs./case
600 cases pork sausages	15000 lbs. Pork Sausage	25 lbs./case	18000 lbs.	30.00 lbs./case
205 cases bologna	5022 lbs. Bologna	24.5 lbs./case	6457 lbs.	31.50 lbs./case
87 cases turkeys	14904 lbs. Turkeys	171.31 lbs. /case	16644 lbs.	191.31 lbs. /case
205 cases lunch meat	5000 lbs. Luncheon Meat	24.39 lbs./case	6435 lbs.	31.39 lbs./case
84 cases chipped beef, in tins	3000 lbs. Chipped beef	35.71 lbs./case	3750 lbs.	44.64 lbs./case
1,147 barrels potatoes **991 crates potatoes**	**301508 lbs. Potatoes**	**141.02 lbs./brl-crte**	**330840 lbs.**	**154.74 lbs./brl-crte**
100 crates onions	10000 lbs. Onions	100 lbs./crate	11700 lbs.	117 lbs./crate
250 tubs butter	15250 lbs. Butter	61 lbs. /tub	18000 lbs.	72 lbs. /tub
500 cases eggs	15000 lbs. Eggs	48.75 lbs./case	30500 lbs.	61.00 lbs./case
526 hlf. bbls. Smoked hams	**47449 lbs. Ham smoked**	**90.21 lbs. /half brl**	**84160 lbs.**	**160.00 lbs. /half brl**
420 cases corned beef, in tins	20160 lbs. Beef corned	48 lbs./case	29400 lbs.	70.00 lbs./case
222 cases bacon, in tins	15984 lbs. Bacon	72 lbs./case	22644 lbs.	102.00 lbs./case
250 cases hams, in tins	6000 lbs./ Ham tinned	24 lbs./case	10000 lbs.	40.00 lbs./case
167 cases salmon, in tins	8016 lbs. Salmon	48 lbs./case	11690 lbs.	70.00 lbs./case
250 sacks sugar	25000 lbs. Sugar	100 lbs./sack	25125 lbs	100.50 lbs./sack

TOTALS

9080 Packages	**812266 lbs.**		**944455 lbs.**	
421 Tons	**[406.13 Tons]**		**[472.2275 Tons]**	

This list of naval provisions headed for Gibraltar was compiled from the *Journal of Commerce*, January 26th, 1909 and the *Memorandum for the Bureau of Supplies and Accounts*, January 25, 1909, NARA RG 143, File 105669.

Note in particular that approximately 90 pounds of ham was carried in 160 pound half-barrels. Added to the ham was 40 pounds of salt per barrel ("... The hams so clothed [in canvas] will be packed in salt, in air-tight half-barrels, containing about 90 pounds of ham and about 40 pounds of hard, dry salt." *--Memoranda for the Information and Guidance of Commandants and Heads of Departments of Navy Yards and Stations Commanding Officers of Ships, Engineering, Navigating, Pay Officers, Etc.* Congressional Information Series ("CIS"), N.2007-1.7, No. 7, Sept. 2, 1902). This leaves 30 pounds for the half-barrel itself. But note that approximately 140 pounds of potatoes were shipped in 14 pound barrels. See Chapter Five.

II.

Balance Sheet for the Great White Fleet's Around-the-World Cruise

Date	Item	Debit	Credit	Balance
22-Sep-08	At sea - Gold in Fleet ($243,133+£47,930)*			$476,384
29-Sep-08	At sea - Gold in Fleet ($230,288+£37,132)*			$410,991
4-Oct-08	Deposit - Manila		$350,000	$760,991
5-Nov-08	Expenditures 9/23 - 11/05	$531,781		$229,210
6-Nov-08	Deposit - Manila		$400,000	$629,210
13-Dec-08	Expenditures 11/06 - 12/13	$519,414		$109,796
14-Dec-08	Deposit - Colombo, Ceylon (£75,000)		$364,988	$474,784
8-Jan-09	Expenditures 12/14 - 01/08	$309,175		$165,600
9-Jan-09	Deposit - Port Said, Egypt (£58,500)		$284,690	$450,290
25-Jan-09	Expenditures 01/09 - 01/25	$197,872		$252,418
22-Feb-09	Expenditures 01/26 - 02/22	$346,276		($93,858)

* Average specified expenditures per month for the entire fleet (as reported) were $371,000, which computes to a daily expenditure of $12,367. The difference between the two reported balances, above, computes to a weekly expenditure of $65,393.48 or $9,341.93 per day. With the Fleet at sea, having departed Albany, Australia on September 18th and arrival at Manila, P.I. on October 2nd, the primary expense would have been the September 25th payroll, with a now computed Fleet payroll of approximately $65,000 per month. Because the primary expense incurred for this period was payroll, the average expenditure for this period would be less because it does not include most operational expenses.

Balance sheet reconstructed from *Operations of Pay Department of the Atlantic Fleet on Cruise Around the World*, Report of Pay Inspector Samuel McGowan, U. S. N. Fleet Paymaster. Presented by Mr. Perkins for Mr. Tillman, June 23, 1910, Congressional Serial 5660, 61st Congress 2nd Session.

Because amounts for "various auxiliaries" and a "usual fleet reserve fund of $42,672.82" were maintained, on-hand cash within the Fleet is not shown to fall below $100,000. Therefore, an analysis of Atlantic Fleet operational data suggests that the Fleet would have required additional funds to avoid a negative balance; in order to maintain at least a $100,000 surplus, the Fleet would have required in excess of $200,000. This amount is in compliance with the amount reported by Mr. Connolly as that which was taken aboard *Republic*.

Certainly, too, the Fleet had also incurred additional and unanticipated cash expenses as a result of its spontaneous participation in the Italian earthquake relief effort; the earthquake took place on December 28, 1908. These additional expenditures are not reflected in the account analysis.

For more details on the the Fleet's operations and payroll expenses, see Chapter Seven.

III.

Gold Import/Export Analysis

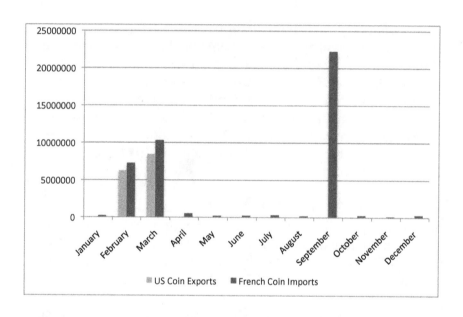

1905	US Coin Exports	French Coin Imports
January	0	$220,564
February	$6,250,000	$7,259,632
March	$8,450,000	$10,318,731
April	0	$525,558
May	0	$215,983
June	0	$240,853
July	0	$335,100
August	0	$210,747
September	0	$22,281,547
October	0	$271,614
November	0	$122,390
December	0	$315,465

I conducted an Import/Export study of gold shipments between the United States and France for the period 1904-1914 (using official government reports supplanted by newspaper accounts). In September of 1905, a very peculiar anomaly was discovered. In that month, France reported a shipment of $22,000,000 in gold coin (an enormous and unprecedented amount during that period of time) received from the United States. However, no corresponding Export report for this amount appears in U.S. Export data. In fact, according to Secretary of Treasury Shaw's remarks in newspapers at the time, banks were recalling their short-term loans in order to send "money to the interior to pay for crops." *Wall Street Journal*, September 2, 1905, 8:2. What actually occurred, the evidence suggests, is that this enormous shipment was made as a result of the Japanese withdrawing their gold from New York to participate in the French markets (perhaps, even, a sub-rosa payment to Russia as part of the settlement of the Russo-Japanese War). This is a specific, and proven instance in which a large shipment of U.S. gold coin was deliberately concealed for political reasons.

A complete list of citations (and more details) can be found on rms-republic.com. Also, see Chapter Eight.

INDEX

Y

CPSIA information can be obtained
at www.ICGtesting.com
Printed in the USA
BVHW06*1421131018
529788BV00001B/4/P